Inheritance

By Charlene Mattson

Copyright ©2023 Charlene Mattson

All Rights Reserved

ISBN: 9798857487846

Cover Art By Elyon
All Rights Reserved

All events and characters portrayed in this book are works of fiction. Any similarities between them and real people and events are entirely coincidental.

Dedication:

As always, thank you to my family for putting up with me locking myself away to write at weird points throughout the day, my boss for encouraging me every November to take part in National Novel Writing Month, and the many book clubs and writing groups I'm a part of that keep me going.

Watch out for Ravens, mirrors, and stick figures in the woods.

Acknowledgements

A lot of research and annoying questions went into this book to make it as true to the area as possible.

Thank you to my brother Kyle Wilson who confirmed a few things for me and made sure I used the *right* terminology for things like fry bread, clans, and other things like that, including slang. (Yes, there is a massive difference between fry bread and bannock! Don't even get my mother started...). I'm sorry I pestered you so much about driving out angry spirits!

Thank you to Aaron Mott who filled in some details about the area for me – I haven't been out west in many years and a lot has changed.

And thank you to my proof-reader who said I *nailed* what life is like as a modern Indigenous person living in the north who has to juggle both working in the modern times and the harsh reality of addictions in the family.

Contents

Contents 7
Prologue 9
Chapter One 15
Chapter Two 30
Chapter Three 40
Chapter Four 60
Chapter Five 75
Chapter Six 92
Chapter Seven 103
Chapter Eight 120
Chapter Nine 128
Chapter Ten 148
Chapter Eleven 157
Chapter Twelve 172
Chapter Thirteen 184
Chapter Fourteen 197
Chapter Fifteen 207
Chapter Sixteen 220
Chapter Seventeen 238
Chapter Eighteen 248

Chapter Nineteen 260

Chapter Twenty 270

Chapter Twenty-One 287

Epilogue 301

Author's Note 306

Prologue

The people of Port Edward had little reason to take the road south. The older canneries were at least temporarily closed, and the woods were starting to reclaim what was once theirs. The Cassiar Cannery Guest Houses were still open, but there were not many tourists now and the locals didn't go there much when they could spend the night somewhere more exotic – Terrace perhaps, or make the longer trip to Prince George, Vancouver, or into Alberta for a long weekend of shopping.

Anyone driving south would have to pass the dirt road leading to the house in the hills and of late people were growing chilled at the thought.

Headlights strobed through the light fog coming off the ocean as the sun set. Music pulsed down the road, a harbinger of humans to come, driving the squirrels back into the trees. The youth driving on the road weren't going anywhere in particular, but they were going to get to nowhere in style.

Startled perhaps by the influx of loud life in its home, a deer suddenly bounded across the road, forcing them to put the brake on things. The car tires squealed in outrage as the driver, a young Ts'mysen man, hauled hard on the steering wheel and slammed the brake pedal hard, trying to avoid the deer which was caught frozen in the headlights. The woman beside him screamed and the younger teen in the back shouted.

Time seemed to shatter as they spun out.

The deer fled and the car ended up in the ditch, tires smoking, the smell of burnt rubber lingering in the air.

"*Shit*," shouted the driver, staggering out of the car and staring at it in horror. "My dad's gonna *kill* me."

"Oh, we're fine, thanks," his passenger said caustically as she climbed out. She opened the back door and helped her boyfriend's younger brother out. He looked more bleary-eyed, though the sight of the tipped-over car in the swiftly growing darkness made his eyes widen.

"How are we going to get the car *out?*" he asked.

"Shit if I know," his brother said, kicking the wheel and cursing again.

"Cell service is down too," his girlfriend commented, checking her phone.

"We'll have to walk back," he said.

The young woman crossed her arms and glared pointedly at her heeled boots. "There's a *driveway* right beside us, you know. It goes to that house, you know, where the white guy lives. We can call for a ride."

"My dad is going to kill me," her boyfriend repeated, but slouched up the driveway, the other two in his wake.

There was a house at the end of the dirt road, but it took almost thirty minutes of walking to reach it. Concerns had been voiced that the owner wouldn't be around, or would be asleep, but the house was brightly lit when they arrived. Marcus glanced behind him; Teri looked relieved to not have to walk anymore and his brother Liam looked worried.

"We'll ask if the guy has a phone and if we can use it," Marcus reassured them. "If he has a cell, we don't even have to go inside."

"Doesn't your dad hunt with this guy?" Teri asked, wincing as her feet reported fresh blisters. "Isn't this Jason's place?"

Marcus sighed. "Yeah, looks like. But then he'll definitely help us out. Maybe he'll even have a way to get the car out of the ditch."

That ray of hope brightened them up and they hurried across the front yard to the door. Marcus knocked and, a few moments later, a taller man with a hint of a gut opened the door. He blinked at them for a moment; in the flickering porch light, his features seemed gaunt, almost skeletal, and his blue eyes shone weirdly. He blinked at them for a moment, his face slid into the relaxed expression of welcome, and Marcus was sure he'd imagined things before.

"Marcus and Liam! What brings you here at this hour?"

"Hi Mr. Marken," Marcus said. "We uh... Can we use your phone? We got into an accident at the bottom of your driveway. Deer on the road. The car went into a ditch."

Jason's expression changed to alarm, and he waved them inside. "Of course you can use the phone. Come in, get cleaned up. Are you alright?"

"My arm hurts," Liam complained.

Marcus shambled his way through the foyer to the phone in the kitchen. He wasn't even sure *who* to call. Putting off his dad's wrath for as long as possible seemed like a very good idea, but he couldn't think of anyone else to call and it would get back to his dad anyway, and then he'd be in even *more* trouble for trying to hide it.

Fortunately for him, the decision was delayed. The phone was out.

"Your phone's not working!" he hollered.

"Sometimes the line goes down," Jason said, helping Liam and Teri into the kitchen. The door to the basement yawned wide on the opposite side of the room. "It should come back in a few minutes. That'll give you time to get cleaned up and for me to get Liam's arm checked. My first aid kid is downstairs with the hunting gear. Follow me."

Liam shot Marcus an uncertain look, but Marcus rolled his eyes at him and waved him on.

They were downstairs for a few minutes while Marcus tried to call his dad a few more times and Teri slouched against the wall, fruitlessly trying her phone. Then Marcus heard Liam scream. He bolted for the basement stairs, Teri behind him.

Most of the basement was an open room, but the room across from the stairs was the butcher room where his dad and Jason, as well as others from the village, processed the meat they hunted. There was no sign of deer or moose now, but Liam was being tied to a hook hanging from the ceiling. He was thrashing as Jason restrained him, but there was something wrong with his eyes; a weird lassitude came over them as though he'd been drugged. His movements were slowing.

"What the fuck are you doing?" Marcus bellowed. "Let go of my brother!"

Jason turned and Marcus skittered to a halt. Teri shrieked.

The taller man had blood streaked down his face and a strange knife in his hand. He was almost lazily slicing through Liam's shirt and chest, blood flowing bright red.

Marcus flung himself at the man and Teri fled back upstairs to try the phone again or her cell phone to call for help.

There was something *wrong* with the kitchen. It was… wavering. She reared back a little, but fear of what was happening in the basement kept her from going back down the stairs. She could hear grunts from Marcus and Jason, and she threw herself onto the table where she had left her phone.

It was still unable to connect to anything and the house line was still dead. She moaned in fear.

There was a final scream from the basement and then a horrible liquid sound.

"Teri..." Jason's voice drifted up the stairs. "Where are you going?"

Gripping her phone hard, Teri fled the room and out the front door. The forest around the house was pitch black, but she staggered through it anyway, the branches lashing at her face and clinging to her dress. She kicked off her boots and ran in her sock feet, breath sobbing in her chest.

Then she tripped and sprawled at Jason's feet. He had followed her and cut her off. She stared up at him in terror.

"Thank you," he said sincerely.

"For what?" she whispered.

"Opening the door," he answered and slashed the knife down into her throat and chest.

***

The missing teenagers were a seven-day wonder for Port Edward, but after the police had investigated the crashed car, and talked to the man living in the house in the hills, it was resolved that they must have wandered into the forest after the accident and gotten lost. There were more investigations and a lot of tears, but the case was closed soon after and the only result was more people warning their children to stay out of the forest and hills.

Chapter One

Books and movies told Evelyn Brody that something dramatic should have happened the day she handed the divorce papers to her drunk husband. There should have been a storm perhaps, or at least some rain. And tears.

The tears refused to come, and her soon-to-be ex-husband was staring blearily at the papers.

"What is it?" he asked as though the words Notice of Family Claim in clear font at the top of the first page weren't clear enough, along with her signatures.

"I've filed for divorce," she said.

"But… but you *can't*," he said, managing to inject a bit of life into his slurred voice.

"I have," she said coolly. "After what happened last week with the boys… I'm not going to keep enabling *this*." She swept an arm around, encompassing the overflowing recycling bins of empty cans, the bottle lying haphazardly across the counters, and the smell of vomit and alcohol that drifted from the bathrooms, despite her best efforts to clean it up. "There are provisions there for visitations contingent on you sobering up. But this isn't *safe*."

Her voice finally cracked, images of her children staring up at her from their hospital beds, her oldest boy with a thick bandage around his shoulder and across his back, where he'd been injured protecting his younger brother from harm. The totalled car was still lying in the impound yard.

I should never have let him take them anywhere. The familiar mantra that had stolen sleep away for the last week played through her mind.

He half-heartedly rifled through the papers, but since he was still badly hung over and rapidly making his way back to drunk, the words made little impression. He shoved them away.

"If you want to fight this in court, go for it, but I think you'll find that judges don't look too kindly on DUIs."

He didn't answer; he already looked defeated.

"You're going to have to start making some choices," she said and barely managed to stop herself from sitting beside him.

You're not his parent, you were his partner, and you're not responsible for his choices! Zan's voice thundered in her head, briefly overpowering the guilt. *Don't let him drag you down with him!*

He didn't answer him, and she didn't really expect him to. She left him there, downing another beer and staring at the shambles of his life.

***

"It's done?"

"It's done," Evelyn confirmed. She was slouched in the chair across from her best friend, staring down at her tea as though expecting it to chastise her for upending her family's life. Upstairs, she thought she heard at least one of her boys trying to eavesdrop, but she didn't have the energy to go upstairs and tell him off.

Zan shook her red-gold hair off her shoulders and smoothed the slightly darker roots with a distracted hand. "It had to be done," she said. "You know it."

"I know," she said. "It was easier after what happened last week. He... He could have *killed* them."

"Simon is a good kid," Zan said. "He kept his little brother safe."

"He shouldn't have had to."

There was nothing Zan could say to that, so she grabbed her mug and poured the last of the tea in it. "What now?"

"I don't know," Evelyn said, raking her fingers through her dark hair. "I can't stay here forever."

"You can stay as long as you need to."

"Zan, the boys are going to drive you up a wall eventually," Evelyn said, smiling weakly. "Besides, they're going to kill each *other* if they share a room much longer. Simon is already grumbling about the lack of personal space and they both say the other one smells funny."

Zan laughed.

"We'll have to find an apartment or something," Evelyn said. "Hopefully I can work enough hours until Robert is forced to pay child support."

She let out a deep sigh. A small part of her wanted to wrap herself around her grief and loss and bury herself in blankets for a month, but the rest of her was too busy planning. She was slightly chilled to realize that she had already consigned Robert to the past and shut the door on him.

It was that knack, to put her feelings aside easily, which Robert claimed had driven him to start drinking and keep other secrets. She never listened to him, he claimed, and never seemed to *emote* in any meaningful way.

She stared down at her tea, wondering, and not for the first time, whether she was damaged in some way. Robert wasn't the first person to have said as much. *Shouldn't I be crying?*

"Yeah, about that," Zan said uneasily. Evelyn snapped out of her reverie and looked at her.

"What?"

Zan huffed out a sigh, her hair falling over her brown eyes as it was wont to do when she had to deliver bad news. "There's a rumor that you're about to be let go."

"*What?!*"

Zan's head bobbed. "I don't know *all* the details." *Which means she knows most of them,* Evelyn thought. "But you know that the bitch in marketing has been gunning for you."

Evelyn scowled. "She can't get me with anything that would stick. I'm one of the best salespeople on the floor. Everyone knows that."

"They're not going to fire you," Zan said. "They're going to lay you off. Apparently, your job has become... redundant."

Evelyn stared at her.

"It's been swirling around for a few weeks now," Zan said, seemingly unable to stop herself now that she'd begun. "But you wouldn't have noticed with Robert being an ass. There are a bunch of mergers happening and they figure they only need a few salespeople to handle things. So, the ones who have been there at least ten years are staying and you're... not."

"But I *know* the tech inside and out! No one else there can answer *half* the questions I can."

Zan held up her hands. "Yeah, *I* know. Except they don't really want you guys answering questions anymore. You know how it's been since covid started; get people in, get people out, especially with the space limits and all. They're shuffling all the questions to the website."

Evelyn seethed. "Which is useless."

"They really don't care. And then the Bitch in Marketing had the brilliant idea to overhaul the whole thing to have remote workers answer questions over chat and social media and..." She shrugged limply.

"And there goes my job and she *wins*."

Zan nodded.

"When?"

"That I don't know," Zan said. "Probably pretty soon. She was looking particularly smug yesterday when you had to call in late because of your appointment with the lawyer."

Evelyn buried her face in her arms. "I *hate* her."

"The feeling has been mutual since prom."

"She can *have* Robert, with my blessings."

Zan laughed. "There would certainly be some poetic justice in that."

Except with my luck, he'd sober up for her.

'Her' being a beautiful, slender, blonde woman who had never pushed babies out of her body and then breastfed them, who enjoyed physical affection, and laughed at all the right jokes. She had made passive aggressive comments about Evelyn ever since the tenth grade, but no one seemed to care too much about that.

Cold, computer-sexual. Bookworm. Walking Wikipedia. Frigid.

Evelyn ground her face into her forearms, trying to bury the taunts, but they hovered in the background, coloring her decision to leave Robert as proof she had no ability to care for someone, not because of his steady decline over the past year.

"You should read a book or watch a movie or try to get some sleep," Zan said a few minutes later when it became obvious that on her own, Evelyn had no intention of raising her head.

"It's been a rough week. I'll get up with Christopher in the morning."

"Thank you, Zan," Evelyn said, managing to lift her head. "You're a great friend."

Zan waved a hand. "The boys are fun."

Evelyn shambled to her small room, which had once been Zan's office and had been hastily redone the week before. It still bore all the marks of a home office, including Zan's current vision board which was splattered with pictures of beaches and airplanes. Evelyn got undressed and collapsed onto the pull-out bed, staring at the ceiling.

No husband – no real loss there, but still – no job soon, no home.

What am I going to do?

Well, for one night at least, she could wrap herself around her grief and anger. It held her for a few minutes, but then her brain ground back to life, contemplating future steps. Any grief over losing her marriage and her job quietly receded in the face of relentless planning.

"Maybe there is something wrong with me," she quietly said to the moonlight slanting through the window.

***

The blue polo shirt itched, and it had never fit her right. No matter how often she was measured, it always bunched up oddly around her stomach and the shoulders drooped. She never liked it. Really, *no one* looked good in it, but she always felt as though she was wearing a sack.

Evelyn tossed the offending garment into the garbage outside her store. The spares were tossed in after it, followed by her name tag.

Zan's predictions for her employment status came true in the form of a polite letter, an even more polite and awkward meeting with HR, and the phone number and website for Employment Insurance with assurances that her record of employment would be ready soon so she could collect EI and... get on with her life.

She was out a job, but at least she didn't have to wear the damn shirt anymore.

Her coworkers had tried to give her a good send-off, but that had been awkward too. There was cake in the breakroom and several of them had signed a card and kicked in for a gift certificate, but it had all underscored how distant they were from her. No one had anything to offer beyond emptying platitudes covering relief that they weren't the ones being handed their notice yet.

"With your skills and knowledge, you'll get another job like *that*," one of her coworkers said brightly, snapping her fingers.

Evelyn hadn't even dusted off her resume yet. She felt unmoored and ready to drift away on an errant breeze. No more blue shirt with the nametag that always poked her in the chest. She would never again have to ask if a customer had tried powering a computer off and on again, if they had checked the task manager.

It was liberating in a horrifying sort of way. She didn't have to set her alarm clock for the morning. It was Monday today, but tomorrow didn't *have* to be Tuesday. Who was going to tell her otherwise? She turned her back on the mall where her store (*Not my store anymore*) was and firmly set herself on the sidewalk leading back to Zan's house. Her best friend had taken the day off work at the main office of her old store, so she would be home with Christopher.

The lawyers had been in touch and Robert had signed everything. There was still the dance of splitting assets, but with the threat that she'd take him to court over the car accident, he'd done everything she demanded as meekly as a kicked dog. It didn't make her feel good, but at least that book was closing without much of a fight.

No job, no husband, no home. The mantra wove around her head, following the rhythm of her footsteps. *No job. No husband. No home.*

No plan.

She shuddered and straightened her spine. She would figure something out. The boys depended on her. And Zan couldn't solve this for her, no matter what she'd say.

A new home first. The boys are going to drive Zan – and each other – crazy soon. The old house had been entirely in Robert's name, something which had made her mother furious, but no bank was going to take a retail worker making a dollar above minimum wage seriously, so that wasn't even on the table. Robert would probably end up selling it to pay for his habits and the child support.

Zan's small house loomed in front of her before she felt ready. The door was flung open to let in the sunshine and what Zan swore was the smell of the ocean. Evelyn only ever smelled Coquitlam: car exhaust, food, and asphalt.

There were giggles and shouts coming from the backyard. Evelyn peered around to see Christopher running after Zan, laughing his head off. Simon was sitting on a bench pretending to read his newest manga, but sneaking peeks at his younger brother, clearly torn between tween disdain and a longing to join. Evelyn knew that feeling as well – she didn't know whether she wanted to be alone or with her children. She compromised, sitting with her oldest son.

"Where's your work stuff?" he asked by way of greeting.

She tousled his dark curly hair. "I'm never wearing that shirt again," she said lightly.

"Oh," he said, wrinkling his nose. "No more discounts on video games then?"

She laughed. "Sorry, Simon."

He shrugged. "It wasn't a very good job, Mom," he said. "They don't treat their people very well."

She smiled a little. Simon was at the age now of knowing that things weren't fair, but young enough to think that something should be done about it. He'd been grumbling about how she and the other salespeople were treated for months.

"Will we go hungry?" he worried.

"No," she said. "I'll look for a better job."

"Dad can help," he said, and the lump that had been successfully kept at bay came back into her throat.

"Yeah," she murmured. "Maybe."

He gave her a sidelong look. "I'm joking," he said flatly. "Dad is sick, isn't he."

"That's one way to put it," she sighed. "I'm sorry, Simon. What happened… shouldn't have happened."

He leaned a little against her and she ran a hand up his back. His shoulders were still bandaged from his injuries, reminding her that he was due for his follow-up appointment in a few days to ensure the stitches were dissolving properly and everything was healing.

"It's okay," he said, correctly interpreting her paused hand. "It doesn't hurt. And Christopher won't remember, will he?"

"I hope not," she said into his curls.

***

The front receptionist knew well why Evelyn and her boys were at the clinic, but she still felt stabs of humiliation over bringing them for Simon's check-up. It was compounded by the fact that she felt as though she had the words 'Laid Off' stamped on her forehead, to go with the feeling that she had betrayed the boys by letting her ex-husband drive them around when she should have known he'd be drunk.

She shut down the feelings of guilt and inadequacy and even managed a smile for the receptionist, who thrust the usual Covid-19 checklist at her and then gestured for them to take a seat.

Christopher grumpily fiddled with his mask until Simon glared at him and then he subsided, though a moment later he was back at it.

"Mom," Simon said.

"Leave it alone, Christopher," Evelyn said automatically. Simon gave his brother a superior look which, being four, he ignored.

"There's no toys," he complained instead, slumping in his chair.

"I know," Evelyn said. "They can't come out right now."

"Simon said there were toys," he grumbled.

"That was before Covid," Simon said with the tone of someone who had said it a dozen times and heard it a hundred more. "Now there's no toys here."

"They'll come back," Evelyn said.

Christopher looked dubious and she couldn't blame him. He didn't remember a time when there *weren't* masks on peoples' faces and constant refrains to wash hands and use disinfectant. He was well accustomed to having his temperature checked every time he was sick and staying home when anyone in the house had a cold.

To Evelyn's mind, it was no way to live, but better than the alternative, and it wasn't as though he knew much different. Simon remembered life without masks, but even that seemed to be growing slightly hazy in his mind.

They didn't have to wait long before being brought into the doctor's examination room. Simon stalwartly removed his shirt so that the doctor could look at the injury while Christopher picked at his mask some more and looked grouchy.

"It's healing nicely," the doctor said. "The stitches are dissolving well and while there will be a scar, it's hardly going to slow you down. How's your head?"

"Fine," Simon sighed. "The bandage on my shoulder is itchy."

"I know," Doctor Julie said gravely. "It won't be on for much longer. We'll book you in one more time in about five days to remove the bandage. Can you move your arms for me? Full circles."

Simon windmilled enthusiastically as though to prove he didn't need the bandages *now*, but pulled a slight face when his arms reached their apex and pulled on the last of the stitches. Evelyn felt a sharp pang in her stomach at that, but she showed no sign of it. Christopher heaved himself on the chair beside her and leaned into her side.

"And how is Christopher doing?" Julie asked, crouching down to meet his dark eyes. "Can I check you?"

"Yeah," Christopher said, though he buried his face in Evelyn's ribs as the doctor prodded his arms, legs, and stomach.

"Does anything still hurt?"

Christopher firmly shook his head and Julie glanced up at Evelyn, her almond-shaped brown eyes speculative.

"Nothing he's complained about," she said. "He's been sleeping, eating, and playing like normal. I thought… I thought there would be more nightmares, but after the first couple of nights, he went right back to his usual self."

"Well, I'm glad to hear that," Julie said, standing up. "The emergency doctors noted that other than some bruising, he seemed fine. The car seat did its job."

"And me too," Simon said. "I held him too. That's what wrecked my shoulder."

Julie smiled at him. "Keeping your little brother safe is one of the most important things you can do," she said warmly. "And you were very strong and brave."

He looked a little mollified by that.

"And you, Evelyn?"

"I'm fine," she said a little too quickly. "I'm not the one who was in a car accident."

Julie cocked an eyebrow at her. "I'm aware," she said. "But it has all been a traumatic experience for you as well. Is there anything you need?"

"No," Evelyn said, giving Simon an evil glance. He was about to open his mouth, probably to ask for a job for her. He glowered, but subsided. "I'm fine, doctor. Thank you."

Julie frowned a little, but she nodded and headed for the door. "I'll let the front know to book you in for a final check and then a follow-up by phone later just to be sure. Soon this will be just a memory."

Simon pelted out the door, but Christopher held Evelyn's hand as they made the final appointment and then walked out into the warmth of the first day of summer. Simon immediately began clamouring for McDonald's, but when Evelyn returned to Zan's with their bags of food, she found she had no appetite for her lunch and Simon was able to make off with her fries uncontested.

Chapter Two

Zan came through the door, ushering in the breeze and the smell of flowers. She looked thoughtful and slightly worried, which for Zan meant a potential catastrophe was looming. Evelyn chewed her lip and felt her stomach drop.

"It's not... I don't think it's all *bad*...?" Zan scrunched up her face and tossed a thick letter to Evelyn, who had been sitting at the table trying to coax Christopher through his lunch. Sensing an opportunity to avoid carrot sticks, the four-year-old slid off his seat and bolted while Evelyn turned the thick letter in her hands.

"What could it be?" Evelyn asked, taking one of the rejected carrots for herself. The envelope was bright yellow with her name on the front, but the return address was for a law firm she'd never heard of in a place she'd never been to, and that only sounded vaguely familiar. She looked questioningly at Zan, who shrugged.

"It's yours anyway," she said. "Open it!"

The top sheet was the important one: a letter from an estate lawyer. Evelyn felt her face pale as she read it.

Greetings Mrs. Evelyn Timms,

I represent Schuester & Myer, Attorneys at Law, based in Prince Rupert, British Columbia. We are writing you to first offer our condolences on the death of your uncle, Mr. Jason Marken. He passed away quietly in his sleep, and he was well taken care of as per his wishes.

We are also writing to you because Mr. Marken left provisions for you in his will. Please find enclosed the information regarding his estate. We will be happy to send a representative to meet with you to discuss the terms in greater detail, or we may discuss this over the phone at your convenience.

Most notably, aside from a sum of money equalling $350,000, Mr. Marken left you a piece of property located south of Port Edward. The property itself has substantial value and we would be happy to help you sell it, if you wish, or you may want to take it for your own. As you will see in the paperwork, it is quite a lovely building, if somewhat rundown, and has held and increased its value in the past five years.

Our condolences again on the death of your uncle and we hope to hear from you soon.

Aaron Myer

Attorney at Law, Estate Lawyer

"Eve, what is it?" Zan asked, but Evelyn found that any words she wanted to say had jammed in her throat upon reading the letter. Instead, she handed it back to Zan and was almost immediately met with a cashier's check, made to the amount noted in the letter, and a stack of paperwork about a house.

"I didn't know you had an uncle," Zan said.

"I do... I mean, I did," Evelyn managed to say around the massive lump in her throat. "But it's been years since I last saw him. He came for the... the wedding. And when Simon was born. But he moved north a while ago and I didn't really know where. We used to talk on the phone once in a while, and he wrote letters, but I haven't spoken to him in a few years now. I didn't even know he'd died." She shrugged. "I didn't think to tell you about him and really, there wasn't much to tell. He was... Well, I guess I *should* say he was kind, but he was a bit of a mean codger at times, and he liked it that way. Definitely a recluse and plenty of people thought he was strange." She laughed a little, but to her surprise, there was a tear running down her face. "He'd been having trouble the last year. Pneumonia. One of the cousins mentioned he'd had a minor stroke. I guess something caught up with him."

"I'm sorry, Evelyn," Zan said.

Evelyn wasn't sure how she felt. A part of her felt sad, but it was a distant thing, as though someone *else* was feeling sad, and she was getting the echoes. She vaguely remembered her uncle as a big, booming man who had large opinions and a large laugh; remembering that made the sadness come closer, touching her eyes and filling her throat. She looked down at the cashier's cheque, as much to distract herself as anything else.

"Nothing about a funeral," Zan said, sounding slightly offended.

"He never wanted one," Evelyn replied, swallowing the lump again. "He always said that if people couldn't get together when he was alive, he was damned if him dying was going to pull them together. It wasn't as though *he* would benefit from it."

Zan laughed.

"He probably asked to be cremated," Evelyn said. "Probably had his ashes scattered on the mountains or something. He had no use for cemeteries and coffins and expensive things like that. He said that once he was dead, there was no point in having a ceremony over his corpse."

"I imagine that offended people," Zan said.

"I'm sure it did," Evelyn said. Her mother hardly ever talked about him, but when she did, it was always in cold, distant tones. "But honestly, I don't know that half of the family well. My dad..." She shrugged. "Well, whatever happened estranged mom from *everyone* on that side and only Uncle Jason talked to me."

Zan put a hand on Evelyn's shoulder. "This does solve a few problems."

"Yeah," Evelyn said. "I was thinking the same thing."

"What will you do with the house?"

"I should at least see it," Evelyn said. "And the boys would probably have fun going on a road trip. Summer vacation starts a bit early this year. The doctor has cleared Simon. We could go, relax in a big house for the summer. He had it up in the hills and near enough to the ocean."

"It would be a nice place to get your head clear," Zan said. "And a summer on the beach sounds like just the way to do it. And you wouldn't even have to worry about working."

"I can decide what to do once I've seen it," Evelyn agreed.

"Just don't move to the wilds of the northwest coast without telling me!" Zan laughed. "I want to see this place too!"

"Of course," Evelyn said.

Now that she had made up her mind, she found that she had a list of things to do and that distracted her from everything else quite ably. She gingerly took the cashier's cheque to the bank where the teller's eyes bulged when she saw it, and for the first time in many years, Evelyn had a hold put on her account while the bank made sure it was legitimate. After being reassured that it would only be held for a few days and that she would be able to access a hundred dollars of it, she then made her calls to the attorneys handling her uncle's estate.

"Mrs. Timms, glad to hear from you," came a mellow voice from the other end of the line. "My name is Shawn Myers."

"It's... Ms. Brody," she hesitantly corrected. "The name change hasn't gone through yet, but I've recently divorced my husband."

There was a pause on the other end and then the voice came back. "Sorry about that," Shawn said. "How can I help you?"

"I wanted to make arrangements to see the house my uncle left me," she said, feeling surreal. "I thought I should call your law firm about it?"

The man chuckled. "My dad and his partner's firm, you mean." He spoke in a rounded accent with laughter coursing the edges. "I'm not even a junior partner yet. But we can make those arrangements. When would you like to see it?"

Evelyn leaned over a bit to see Zan's slightly psychedelic calendar hanging on the wall. "In a week? Would that work?"

There was the rustle of paper on the other end and the scratching of a pen. "That's fine," the man said warmly. "We're based out of Prince Rupert, but we'll send someone to meet you at Port Edward, which is much closer to the property, and then lead you from there. The road to the house is kind of rough, just to warn you. The post office is probably the best place to meet. It's right on the road into the village coming in from the Terrace side."

"Thanks," Evelyn said, a little startled at how swiftly she'd been swept into the man's planning.

"See you in a week, Ms. Brody."

Evelyn nodded, forgetting for a moment that of course the man couldn't see her, but there was already a click from the other end.

"Zan!" she called. "Where the hell is Port Edward other than 'north'?"

***

Packing up their lives was easy when most of it had been left in shambles and behind them. The hardest part had been convincing the boys to leave some of their things with Zan and make sure they all had new socks, underwear and clothing for the trip north. Upon doing further research, Evelyn quickly realized that they would be on the road for upwards of twenty hours to reach their destination and that meant at least one motel stay and the very real chance of bored children.

"There might be whales," Simon said enthusiastically. "Your uncle lived by the ocean, didn't he?"

"Well, sort of," Evelyn said, squinting at her phone, trying to find their destination. "There are a lot of islands up there and they're all clustered together. If I'm understanding this, he lived across from the Lelu and Smith Islands. I don't know if whales would really travel the inlets."

"Whales!" Christopher repeated and Evelyn gave up on trying to let them down gently about the low probability of regularly seeing whales.

Her ex-husband had totalled the car in the accident, but she still had her older SUV, and she was grateful that she'd dug her heels in and bought it, despite teasing from her friends and predictions from her mother that she'd never be able to afford it on retail wages. She may not have a lot now, but it was much easier to pack up an SUV than it would have been to fit everything in a standard car.

"I hope the house is furnished," she sighed, her hands on her hips as she watched her sons trudge out with their suitcases and bags. "Even if I wanted it all, I could hardly bring the furniture with me."

"You wouldn't want it anyway. It's probably all stained and I bet Robert trashed a lot of it," Zan pointed out.

"You're probably right," Evelyn said.

"Well," Zan said, buckling Christopher into his car seat and ruffling his hair. "That looks to be about it."

"Yeah," Evelyn said. "Pretty pathetic that the past eleven years of my life fits in an SUV with room to spare, don't you think?"

"The important things fit in there," Zan said, cocking her head at Simon and Christopher who were blessedly, and probably only momentarily, sharing the Switch. "That's all that matters. Take care of yourself out there, Evelyn. Call me when you get to… Where are you staying tonight?"

"Prince George," Evelyn said. "It's the last major city on the route and about halfway to Port Edward. And the hotel we're staying in has a pool for the boys."

Zan gave her a hug. "Be careful Evelyn, but also… Try to enjoy yourself. Take the summer to regroup."

"Thanks for everything, Zan," Evelyn returned.

She kept her best friend in her rear-view mirror for as long as possible, and then set her vehicle on the highway and began driving.

Evelyn had never been beyond Hope, so as the sun pushed itself into a bright June morning, she felt the fine combination of nerves and excitement that came from going somewhere brand new. The highway was busy, but level and easy to drive, and as they turned north after Hope, the scenery grew wilder: more mountains and wide rivers that crashed below the highway. There were fewer cars on the road by the time they reached Lillooet, and more birds. Even the boys stared wide-eyed as they drove beneath the shadows of the mountains and through villages.

"It's so different," Simon said, his nose glued to the window. Christopher had lost interest and gone back to his toys, but Simon was enthralled by the river following their road.

They pulled into Prince George shortly before dinner and even though it was hailed as BC's Northern Capital, the city was smaller than Coquitlam, let alone Vancouver. Their hotel was just off the main highway coming in, behind the looming figure of a strange man who looked to be made of a giant log, holding a flag, and smiling benevolently at people coming into the city.

"What is that?" Christopher asked through a yawn.

"Mr. PG," Evelyn said, smiling a little. She pulled into the main parking lot of the hotel and helped Simon and Christopher get out. They shook out the cramps of nine hours on the road and then ran, yelling, for the pool.

The boys collapsed into sleep after dinner, the pool, and the general excitement of the road trip caught up with them. Evelyn, though, found that she couldn't get comfortable on the new bed with the city growing strangely quiet around her save for the rumble of logging trucks. Coquitlam was never quiet, and the city was always bright. While there were lights in the parking lot and a slight haze of light over the main city, when she looked outside, she could also see the stars more brightly than she ever had in the lower mainland. She leaned against the window.

I don't know if I feel relieved, excited, or scared.

If she didn't get some sleep, she would mostly just feel exhausted in the morning, and it was another eight or nine hours to Port Edward. She left a voice mail for Zan, telling her they were safe in Prince George, and then forced herself to lie down in bed. She used her boys' rhythmic breathing to lull herself to sleep.

Chapter Three

Shawn Myer was dutifully trying to listen while his father talked to him about Ms. Brody's arrival, but his mind was wandering to the fishing boats on the coast and the great ships beyond them. The water would be plentiful with Chinook and Coho salmon and, even though he rarely kept anything he caught, the idea of being out on the water was more enticing than the office. The fact that it was a rare sunny day in Prince Rupert didn't help to keep his attention where it was supposed to be.

"Shawn," his father said, an edge to his voice.

"Sorry," he sighed. "Ms. Brody, arriving today."

"Her uncle was an excellent client, and a friend, and we want to make sure his wishes are carried out," his father said, heaving a sigh and leaning back in his chair. His black hair was threaded with gray and the wrinkles around his dark eyes deepened as he contemplated the waters below his window. "I still can't quite believe he's dead."

Shawn laid his hands on the desk. "I'll make sure everything is sorted out," he said. "You're right to send me. I know where the place is, and it makes as much sense for me to go as anyone else."

"You have all the information you need, and the keys," his father said, seeming to come back to himself. "If it weren't for having to work on the briefing for the lawsuit against those bastard commercial fishers, I'd be doing this myself."

"You have to keep fighting the fight here," Shawn said. "Besides, you're getting too old to be running around the mountains."

His father snickered. "This will be a good experience for you."

"I'll do my best," Shawn said. "*Nm al gyik niidzn.*"[1]

His father raised an eyebrow, impressed. "Studying *sm'algyax*?"

"A little," Shawn said. "For *Nts'T'its.*" [2] He stumbled a little over the word and his father smiled.

"Your grandmother would have approved. Now, get going, you have to make sure you have everything."

For once, there was still no sign of impending rain and Shawn took that as a good omen. He unlocked the door of his jeep and swung in, tossing a regretful look to the fishing gear in the back. There was no chance he'd be able to use it today, and it would probably stay unused for a few more days while Evelyn settled in. He checked his reflection to make sure his thick black hair wasn't tufting in all directions on him, as it was

---

[1] Sm'algyax for "See you later". https://www.smalgyax.ca/greetings

[2] 'Grandmother' https://www.smalgyaxword.ca/

wont to do when the wind got to it, and then put the jeep in drive and headed out of Prince Rupert, south to Port Edward.

Port Edward was small, but it was close to the water with a large harbor and plenty of boats and ships. There was a massive hill backing the village, a precursor to the Coast Mountains beyond. The village was in the throes of cleaning itself up and becoming green and beautiful, but Shawn knew where to look to find the old underbelly of houses that were growing steadily more dilapidated. And while village council advertised the village's quaint loveliness, Shawn was sure that there were fewer people he knew every year. Everyone was slowly leaving for Prince Rupert, Terrace, Prince George, or even further afield: Vancouver or out east.

Or, nearly as often, they went to Prince Rupert and never left, quietly interred in the cemetery.

He pulled his jeep up to the small post office and hopped out, giving the vehicle a pat. The road to Jason's house was narrow and winding; he hoped that Evelyn had a vehicle that could handle it. There was no sign of a worried stranger yet, so he took a deep breath of ocean air and resigned himself to waiting.

His mind turned to events of the past, as it often did when he came home. He didn't explore around Port Edward much anymore. The woods and mountains were deep, dangerous, and strange. It wasn't only twisted truckers and cops who took victims from the villages.

Less than a year ago, three teens had gone missing and only their car was found in a ditch. A year before that, it had been two tourists doing the Cannery drive who disappeared after leaving the old Northern Pacific. Their car had been found parked, as politely as one pleased, on the side of the road, but they had never been found. And the year before that, while he was finishing university in Ottawa, it had been two of his own cousins who had gone missing. Their car was found a smoking wreck, so everyone assumed they'd wandered off in a daze and been killed by a bear. His dad's youngest sister, having lost her children, was never the same again and died the very next year on the anniversary.

So far, only Shawn seemed to be concerned about the fact that there had been *several* strange disappearances, all on the road going south from Port Edward, and he wasn't interested in being added to the list. His cousin had been a careful driver and he couldn't imagine them wrecking the car on their own. But he'd been far away at the time, and he hadn't been able to fight the point. By the time he returned, it was an old tragedy which was something everyone was used to.

He shook himself. *Seeing patterns where there are none,* he scolded himself. It was true that the land out here could be deadly; there was nothing beyond Port Edward except trees, hills, and mountains; moose, bear, and the occasional cougar and wolf. There were plenty of places to get lost and even in the middle of summer, it could get chilly at night and very wet. One didn't have to run afoul of anything weird to go missing and get killed – a moose, bear, or bad run from bugs could do it.

He gave the woods around the village a mistrustful look anyway.

***

Heading west from Prince George, the road quickly grew thin, and the mountains began to creep in close. They left early enough that the front desk warned them of moose and bear on the roads, but much to the disappointment of the boys, they saw nothing but logging trucks. Between the thick trees, mountains, and the river that followed their road from Telkwa on, the boys were enraptured.

"It even *smells* different here, Zan," Evelyn murmured. No chemicals, pollutants, or other things she'd always taken for granted. The air was crisp and smelled of nothing worse than trees.

It was still uncomfortable. They drove for hours, seeing little more than small towns with nothing between those small outcrops of civilization but the road, mountains, trees, and occasional pasture given over to cows. The signal on her smartphone was patchy, often fizzling out for long minutes. If they broke down on the road, it could be hours before anyone would come across them to help. She shivered and tried not to think about it, her grip tightening on the steering wheel.

The small town of Hazelton whipped by in the blink of an eye and they were back on the road with Evelyn keeping an eye on her phone's Google maps, which informed her that the next major town, so to speak, was Terrace. The boys were getting cranky with their snacks and breakfast had worn thin after almost six hours on the road.

"We'll stop in Terrace," she promised. "And after that, it's less than two hours to Port Edward."

Despite this promise, she still endured over an hour of them grousing at each other over the Switch, their toys, and their books before they finally pulled into town. She found an A&W to eat burgers and fries and stretch their legs.

Terrace was a low-slung town, huddled between the mountains and the river. It did smell like pulp mill here, but it was easy to ignore. Many of the buildings were scattered between empty lots and there was the vague feeling of transience in the air – even people didn't want to settle roots in the thin soil.

"Everything is so far apart up here," Simon commented. "It's not like at home."

"I know," Evelyn said, putting an arm around his shoulders. It was reassuring to not feel bandages under his shirt anymore. "It's very different here, isn't it?"

Christopher swung his legs on the bench and took a big bite of his burger. "I wanna see bears and mooses," he said.

"I'm sure we will," Evelyn said. "My uncle's house was a bit far away from any towns, so there will be more wildlife."

Christopher looked happy, but Simon looked more dubious. "Moose are really big, aren't they?" he said. "I'd rather see whales."

"Whales are big too," Evelyn pointed out, chuckling.

"But they don't come on *land*," Simon said, rolling his eyes at his mother and devouring his fries. "Moose charge at people."

"We'll just have to be careful," Evelyn said.

After they finished their lunch, Evelyn stopped at the grocery store to buy essentials, figuring that the house would be emptied of food. At the very least, she didn't want to face the next morning without coffee, cereal, and a few easy meals so that she could keep them all from getting too cranky while she sorted out the lay of the land. Then they piled back into the SUV and headed west again, following the river to where it would empty into the sea.

She was worried she wouldn't be able to find Port Edward, but the road only forked once in order to go to Prince Rupert. The road turned south when it hit the coast and dropped her off at the smallest village she'd been through yet.

A massive hill overlooked the village, the sound of the ocean a heartbeat of life. The waves lapping against the harbor were pervasive and the small houses hugged greenbelts and narrow roads. The largest building was what looked to be a school, but she couldn't be sure.

The post office was easy to find and there was only one person in the parking lot, leaning against a dusty black jeep. She pulled up several feet away.

"Stay here," she warned her boys. They glowered at her, sensing a missed opportunity to run around, but obeyed, while she got out and cautiously walked towards the man waiting by his vehicle.

He was clearly Indigenous with his thick black hair and coppery brown skin. He had dark, friendly eyes, and was wearing a suit jacket, but also beat up jeans, as though he'd been hoping to not be at work, but somehow knew he would likely be stuck with it. He grinned at her, his teeth shockingly white, and held out a hand for her to shake.

"I'm Shawn Myers," he said, and she recognized his voice from the phone call the week before. "Ms. Brody?"

"Yes," she said, accepting his hand and marvelling slightly at how firm it was. The divorce lawyer she was working with was good at his job, but his handshake was always limp.

Shawn also looked a few years younger than her, and she felt weirdly ashamed of the fact that she was a laid off retail worker and someone younger than her was a lawyer.

He leaned against his jeep. "Find your way okay?"

"Yeah," she said. "It's a much longer drive than I thought it was. We left Coquitlam early yesterday and Prince George first thing this morning and it's already getting well into the afternoon!"

He nodded. "It's a lot different up here than Vancouver, eh?"

"I was worried we would break down and get stranded," she admitted. "There are too many places without cell service."

"You get used to it," he said. "They keep saying they'll bring more service up here, but it hasn't happened yet." He smiled as though laughing at an inside joke, but Evelyn didn't think it was funny. "Do you need some time to stretch? Your uncle's house isn't far from here, and it'll be light for a while yet."

Evelyn glanced at the boys who were practically plastered to the window, staring at the man she was talking to. "Probably a good idea," she said and let the boys out of the vehicle. They came out like twin shots, though Christopher was quickly overcome with shyness.

"I'm Simon," her oldest said, holding out his hand for Shawn to gravely shake. "And this is Christopher. He's just being dumb."

"'m not," Christopher mumbled.

"Happy to meet you," Shawn said. "*Ama gawdi suulgyaxs.*"

Christopher peered up at him. "What does *that* mean?"

Shawn grinned. "It means 'Good afternoon', in Sm'algyax, which is the language of my people." He crouched down to eye level with Christopher and Evelyn was amused to see Simon copy him, his dark blue eyes wide. "If you want to say hello back, you can just say '*niit*'. That means 'hello'."

"*Niit*," Christopher whispered, tripping over the unfamiliar word. Simon tried as well and did a little better, earning a broader grin from the lawyer.

"We'll make speakers of Sm'algyax out of you yet. No one will believe you're white." He chuckled to himself and then stood up and flashed Evelyn a slightly apologetic and somehow smug look. She grinned back, finding herself oddly charmed by him.

"Your uncle's old house isn't far, but it is up in the hills. Can your SUV four by four all right?"

"As long as the road isn't too steep," she said uncertainly.

"Let's go then. Did you need to buy groceries?"

"I bought some in Terrace."

"Good," Shawn said. "There's not much here. Most people go to Prince Rupert."

"Are there video games in Prince Rupert?" Christopher asked.

"There's a Walmart," Shawn offered.

"You'll manage with what you have," Evelyn said, and Christopher pouted.

"Let go before it gets dark," Shawn said, swinging into his jeep. Evelyn herded the boys back to her SUV and followed Shawn through the village and out, going south, the ocean's edge on one side, and the trees closing in on the other.

The water quickly disappeared from view as the trees grew in around them. Shadows began stripping the road, cast by the hills.

As promised, they didn't have to travel far before they were turning onto a rough and narrow road going up into the hills. It looked as though it had only been barely cut through – the worrying whack of tree branches were a constant companion as they traveled. The boys, sensing that their mother was trying to concentrate, stayed quiet, their faces turned to the windows as the light grew dim.

Finally, the trees and road broke into a wide clearing and, in the middle of it, the house that Evelyn had inherited. The jeep crunched to a stop in a rough parking space and Evelyn pulled up beside him.

"Well," Shawn said, digging the keys out of his pocket. "This is it."

Thrilled to be out of the vehicle after a seventeen-hour trip, the boys clambered out and ran around, calling out to each other and shrieking across the clearing. Evelyn stood back and bit her lip.

The house had probably been stunning ten years ago. A wide staircase went up to double doors with a large front porch and three arches looping from the porch rails to the overhanging roof. The second storey had huge windows that stared out at them, and even what looked like an attic window under a peaked roof. The area under the porch was fenced off with lattice work that was still mostly white in color.

The overall neglect of the house was obvious, though. The woodwork around the windows was splintering, the glass was grimy. The paint on the house had faded to a dirty dark blue and the few curtains were torn and sagging. Oddly, the grass was well trimmed and there were what looked like carefully tended rose bushes around the front steps.

"There's a greenhouse in the back," Shawn said, consulting his tablet. "And a basement that's finished. The greenhouse should still be in good shape, though I guess we'll see."

"Is someone still doing yard work?" she wondered, looking at the thick rosehips.

Shawn glanced over and shrugged. "Maybe? Your uncle didn't mention anything, but it might not have occurred to him to do so. Something to keep an eye on anyway. Whoever it was probably won't be coming back now that their employer is dead."

Evelyn slowly made her way to the house. She didn't know why, but the isolation combined with the shabbiness of the place made her uneasy, though her boys were thrilled with the find. She looked up at where the porchlight should have been, but only a gaping hole met her eyes.

Shawn sighed. "It's a fixer," he admitted. "I don't think your uncle had the energy to do much with it before he died, and the groundskeeper, assuming there was one, was probably only hired to worry about the yard. But the bones, as a friend of mine says – she's in real estate – are sound, and the locks are good. I checked them myself."

"I think it's cool," Simon said, finally coming to a halt with Christopher behind him. "Like a ghost story."

Evelyn shuddered. "There are no ghosts here," she said firmly. "But it's going to be dark soon. We should get inside."

Shawn unlocked the door with a flourish and waved them inside, tossing Evelyn the keys. The boys tried to dart around their mother, but she blocked them.

The inside was nearly as gloomy as the outside, but at least, when she flipped the switch, the hall light flickered to life. It didn't illuminate much to give her confidence. There was a foyer with a dusty rug leading her eyes to an open room in the near distance. A staircase curled its way around the right-hand wall going up to the second floor. The light came from a dusty chandelier hanging from the ceiling.

"There's nothing living here," Shawn reassured her. "My dad had exterminators come through here to get rid of any pests that may have tried to move in."

That was a relief; at least she wouldn't have to worry about mice or rats, but she still cautiously made her way to the open room on the far end and turned on the lights there. Once that room, which had to be the living room judging from the plastic wrapped couches, the dark blue recliner, an ornately carved coffee table, and a clean but empty fireplace, was lit up, she was able to relax a little.

"The kitchen is just over there," Shawn said, gesturing to a pair of doors with glazed windows. "Upstairs has three bedrooms and a master bedroom with an ensuite, plus the attic room that was used for storage. There are still a few boxes up there, but you could clean it up and use it for something else. Main bathroom is over there," he waved at a smaller door on the left wall off the living room. "The basement has a pretty large empty room that wasn't used for much of anything." He glanced around, but the boys were still frisking in the foyer, and he dropped his voice.

"You'll find one room that will seem weird downstairs. It's the old butcher room. All that's left in there is the old main drain in the middle and the steel sinks and counters, plus maybe a few hanging hooks. Your uncle used to hunt moose up here with my family and a few others, and they'd do some of the processing here."

Evelyn shuddered a little.

Shawn shrugged. "Otherwise, not a bad space really: four bedrooms, a big bathroom and an ensuite, lots of storage, a greenhouse. Close to the mountains and the ocean."

"I don't think we'll be able to move here permanently," she said. "There's nowhere for the boys to go to school close by."

"There is a school in Port Edward, but it only goes to grade four," Shawn admitted. "After that, they'd be going to Prince Rupert. And... it's a pretty small school. Prince Rupert isn't far from here, though. It's only about a fifteen-minute drive once you're back on the road."

"And no jobs for me," Evelyn said, smiling faintly. "This was more for the trip. Then I can decide what to do with this place. Probably sell it, I guess." She felt a pang at that. It was a touch creepy and shabby, but it did remind her of her uncle.

Shawn nodded. "Do you need anything else from me now? Otherwise, I should be getting back to Rupert. My dad will want me to check in."

"Thanks, but I don't think so," Evelyn said, gesturing for the boys to come say their farewells. Shawn shook their hands again and passed Evelyn a business card.

"If you think of anything you need," he said. "Don't hesitate to call. The firm is at your disposal." He grinned again. "I can also point you in the direction of a good realtor."

"Thanks," Evelyn said again, and he smiled and left. A moment later, she heard the jeep start, and the crackle of gravel being driven on as he returned to the main road.

"It's a really big house," Shawn said enthusiastically. "I don't have to share a room with Christopher anymore!"

Christopher looked less happy about that.

"Let's see what the bedrooms look like first," Evelyn warned. "They might not be fit to sleep in."

To her surprise though, when they opened up the bedrooms, nothing more sinister greeted her than the smell of dust with a residual chemical tang from the exterminators. The beds were a bit dusty, but the blankets and sheets that were folded in large cedar chests in the closets were perfectly clean. Evelyn gave them a relieved look and made the beds for the boys. Then they trouped back downstairs to open the kitchen and figure out something to eat.

The oven worked, though there were only the basics for cooking implements. Evelyn went back outside, shivering in the mountain air, unloaded the food, and brought it all back in. They would have to eat a simple meal tonight but given that they had eaten a late lunch and the boys looked exhausted, grilled cheese was probably all anyone would want. While she cooked, Simon brought in more of their bags and then they ate supper.

"We can explore more tomorrow," Evelyn said, correctly gauging her boys' states as they slumped in their chairs. "Bed now."

They were too tired to argue the point as they followed her to their rooms. Simon fell face first into his mattress and then rolled over and stared at the wooden bedposts. "I've never had a four-poster bed. Only read about them."

"Do you like it?" Evelyn asked, tucking him in.

"It's neat," he yawned. "I hope there's room for my stuff."

Evelyn glanced around the room, which was much larger than Simon's old one, and certainly larger than the one he'd shared with Christopher at Zan's. "I don't think there's much danger of your stuff not fitting."

He yawned again and rolled away from her, a clear indication that it was time for her to tuck in his brother.

Christopher was less comfortable. He bounced uneasily on the mattress.

"This place is dark," he announced when Evelyn came in. "I don't know if I like it."

"Do you want me to sleep in here tonight?"

He considered that, his worries about the dark and being in a new place clearly warring with the fact that he though Simon would make fun of him for wanting their mother to stay. Pride won. "I'm not a *baby*."

"Of course you aren't," Evelyn said, hiding a smile while he defiantly lay down. "My room is just across the hall though. If you think *I* might need protection from something."

He nodded and started yawning. The long days of driving, combined with the burst of running around the house had done him in. She tucked him in and then slipped out and across the hall to the master bedroom.

It was far larger than any other bedroom she'd ever had and not only did it boast a large bed, but also a writing desk, two empty bookcases, and two large chests, also full of blankets. She couldn't quite bring herself to do more than sit on the bed and instead stared out the back window at the darkening mountains and trees.

Call Zan, she reminded herself. Fortunately, there was cell service here, improved slightly by sitting right by the window, though there were still fewer bars than she was comfortable with.

"Well?" Zan greeted her. She sounded slightly muffled, but Evelyn didn't know whether that was from something she was doing or from a reduced signal. "How's it going? I got your voice message, but it was pretty light on the details."

"We got here fine, the boys didn't kill each other," Evelyn said. She was watching the shadows grow over the greenhouse until they devoured the small building. "We're at the house now."

"And?"

Evelyn turned away from the window, unwilling to watch the last of the light fade. "Uncle Jason couldn't keep it up," she said. "It needs work. But it's not leaking or anything and there's no vermin, so it's liveable."

"But?" Zan prompted. She could always tell when Evelyn was worried, apparently even from over a thousand kilometres away.

"Nothing really," she sighed. "Nothing I can put my finger on. I think with some work, it will probably sell well. Mostly paint and replacing a few things. I could probably hire people from Prince Rupert to do whatever I can't."

"Are you close to the ocean?" Zan asked eagerly.

"I guess so, but up here in the hills, you can't see it," Evelyn said. "We drove by it, though, and Port Edward and Prince Rupert aren't far from here. The house is in a clearing in the hills and forest, so no ocean view."

Zan snapped her fingers. "Still, it sounds lovely," she said. "A great place for the boys to run and yell their hearts out all summer. And you won't have to think about your mom or Robert getting underfoot."

"I don't have to worry about *anyone* getting underfoot," Evelyn said, trying to laugh. "The lawyer handling the estate is a twenty-minute drive away and the closest village is Port Edward and it's *tiny*. I don't think I have any neighbors at all." She shivered. If things went wrong, she'd be on her own.

She had never *truly* been on her own before. She wasn't sure what to make of it.

"I suppose the lawyer is some stuffy old fart," Zan said sadly.

She'll find out eventually, Evelyn told herself. "No, he's about our age, maybe a bit younger." She could practically see Zan perk up. "Maybe an inch under six feet, black hair, dark eyes, skin like copper. You'd have hearts in your eyes over him."

Zan cackled.

"Simon likes him," Evelyn said thoughtfully. "I wasn't sure he'd trust anyone for a while, but Shawn made him open up a little."

"Out of the mouths of babes," Zan said. "Though I've heard things about the amount of drinking that goes on up there."

Evelyn shrugged. "He was sober. And there's not a lot else to do up here. The closest actual town, other than Prince Rupert, is an hour away. Prince George is the only city up here – and it's smaller than Coquitlam by the way – and it's *eight* hours away. Maybe all people can do is work and then drink for fun."

She knew Zan was pursing her lips. The other woman took the idea of 'my body, my temple' very seriously and rarely even let caffeine pass her lips, though she never begrudged anyone else having it. But she had never approved of alcohol and Robert's descent into whiskey, beer, and rum had only cemented her feelings on the whole thing.

"Anyway," Evelyn said hastily before either of them could take a nasty walk down memory lane. "If Shawn *does* drink, he wasn't doing it while at work. He was friendly and left me his number in case I need something."

"Like a tall, black-haired man to work around the house." Zan had clearly managed to snap herself from the precipice of a dark mood.

Evelyn snorted.

"You should focus on enjoying yourself this summer," Zan said. "Relax, paint some rooms, play with the boys. Go to the ocean a lot."

"I will," Evelyn said. "I'll call again in a few days."

"Let me know how things go with Shawn," Zan said slyly, and Evelyn hung up on her laughter.

Shaking her head, Evelyn turned back to the window. The light behind her cast her own reflection on the glass as a watery ghost, faded and worried. She looked beyond it, letting her eyes unfocus.

Something moved across the grass. A shadow, a flickering shape that looked almost like a person.

But when she blinked and looked again, it was perfectly still outside.

Chapter Four

Evelyn woke up slowly and uncomfortably. The bed was wrong – too large and too stiff. It took a moment for her memories to come back, and even when they did, she wasn't sure what to do with them.

A large house in the woods and a bank account that means I don't have to worry about the bills for a while.... But...

Her brain spluttered at the fact that one of her family had *died*, and it demanded coffee instead. She could hear the boys stirring in the rooms across the hall from her.

It was chilly in the early morning in the mountains, but the sun was already rising and promising a warm day. The house felt a lot less intimidating with the sun beaming in through the windows, though it also looked *more* shabby. She shambled down the stairs and was extremely thankful that a working coffee machine had been left behind, or, judging from how new it looked, purchased on her behalf, perhaps by the law firm. The boys wandered down after her; Simon looked sleepy, but Christopher looked fearful.

"I had bad dreams, mama," he said, leaning against her legs.

She stroked his dark hair. "I'm sorry to hear that, baby. What about?"

"I don't know," he said sadly. "But they were scary."

"Dreams can't hurt you," she said, crouching down. "But they can be scary. Go outside in the sun for a few minutes. That will make the last of the bad dreams go away."

Christopher nodded and stood outside the back door, watching the sun send fingers of light through the trees. "No mooses or bears," he reported. "But I saw a squirrel."

Simon rolled his eyes. "There were squirrels in Coquitlam too," he pointed out. "That's not a big deal."

"It was a big squirrel," Christopher argued, coming inside. "With a big bushy tail."

Simon was unimpressed. "I want to see the greenhouse," he said. "And the trees. Can I go for a walk today?"

Evelyn bit her lip and looked out the kitchen window. It was calm, but the trees were deep, and she didn't know her way around at all. On the other hand, she couldn't keep Simon locked in the house all summer. That would undo the reason for bringing them here in the first place.

"Be careful," she said. "And don't go far. Make sure you can always see the house."

"I will," Simon said. He grabbed some toast and went outside, glaring at his younger brother who tried to follow him. Christopher gave him an offended look and returned to his cereal, sulking. Evelyn ruffled his hair.

"You would have been bored anyway," she said. "Simon will be looking for bugs and plants and things. He'd just get grouchy with you."

Christopher heaved a sigh. "I don't know what to do."

She finished her coffee and grabbed her own toast. "We'll take Simon to the beach later and you can look for shells if you want. It looks like it will be a nice day today."

"Okay," Christopher said, brightening up enough to finish his breakfast and go upstairs to pull his toys out of his bag.

There was a knock at the front door and Evelyn looked up, startled. It was probably just someone who wasn't aware that her uncle was dead, but she gave the front door a deeply mistrustful look as she made her way to it and peered around the edge.

"Marnin'," Shawn said cheerfully. "I had some time before dad wanted me to work with him on a deposition, so I thought I'd see how you were getting on after your first night."

Who else would it have been? She scolded herself and opened the door wider. "Good morning, Shawn. Would you like some coffee?"

"Thanks," he said and made his way past her. "Place looks a little less scary by day."

"Some cleaning and repairs will help," she said, leading him back to the kitchen and pouring him a cup. Christopher peered around the corner of the door and inched his way into the room.

"*Niit*," he said, and Shawn's grin grew wider.

"*Ama ganlaak,*" Shawn answered. "That means 'Good morning'. You've been practicing!"

Christopher smiled a little, looking proud. He didn't stay for long though, even basking in Shawn's praise couldn't stand up against his toys. Shawn took a swig of his coffee as the younger boy pelted away.

"I didn't hear him practicing," Evelyn said thoughtfully. "I think he might have a bit of a knack for languages."

"I'm happy to pass it along," Shawn said. "My grandmother was teaching me before she died." He looked a little sheepish. "I forgot a lot of it and decided to pick it back up a few months ago." He took another swallow. "Sleep okay? No bears or moose tramp through the yard?"

"Not that I saw," Evelyn said, starting to wish she had told Simon to stay in the house after all. Shawn chuckled at her discomfort.

"I'm teasing you," he said. "This time of year, there's no reason to come anywhere near a house when there's food everywhere else. Just keep your garbage contained."

Evelyn still felt uneasy, but she pushed it aside. "We're probably going to need to do some actual shopping for food soon," she said. "And I wanted to take the boys to the beach."

"Prince Rupert for both," Shawn said amiably. "Better shopping to be had there and plenty of beach for the boys to run on. I'm on my way back, so stop by the office if you think of anything you need. Thanks for the coffee!" He tipped his head a little at her and headed back out.

Evelyn put the cups in the sink, but she didn't have the energy to start washing up. Instead, she went back to her room, unpacked a few books, and stared out the window. She could see the brush moving where Simon was poking around and heard Christopher talking to himself in his room.

It should have all felt very idyllic, but it was also very quiet. She didn't even hear any vehicles on the road, though she knew that they weren't far away.

Her eyes slid over to her phone, but no one had called either. The last correspondence regarding the divorce had been on the lawyers' sides and since Robert wasn't really fighting for anything, her lawyer suspected it would all go smoothly. There was still ICBC to deal with since the car had been totalled and would be written off, but since Robert had been DUI, he wasn't going to see a cent in claims. She had nothing to do with that beyond giving a statement – the vehicle had been entirely in Robert's name.

It wasn't that long ago that I was still working at the store and married. Now I'm out in the middle of nowhere, about to be divorced, and nowhere to get a job around here, even if I wanted one right now.

That was reason enough to feel uneasy, she supposed, but something about the place pressed on her temples as well. She shook herself. *It's quiet and new to you,* she scolded herself. She then stood up, told Christopher to get his things together to go to the beach, and went outside to call for Simon.

The best way to combat quiet was to go somewhere teeming with life again.

***

The woods around their new house were mostly made up of different fir and spruce trees, making the transition from the morning brightness of the yard to the cool shadows abrupt. They reared well above Simon, their bark gnarled and thick against the cold and wet winters. There were the sounds of woodpeckers and bird song around him, but he didn't see anything much larger than the squirrels Christopher was crowing about. The ground was thick with old tree needles and there were roots poking out of the earth, creating their own tripping hazards. The air smelled wet and green.

Simon moodily kicked some pinecones. He wasn't sure why he had been so grumpy with his younger brother, but being outside on his own forced him to confront the fact that he wasn't sure how happy he was with all of this. He was still angry at his father for getting them into such a bad car accident (especially after he had *told* his dad that he shouldn't be drinking and driving and his dad just ruffled his hair and told him not to worry about it, fumes wafting off his breath). But being angry at his dad didn't mean he wanted to be over a thousand kilometres away from him either, even if it was just for the summer.

There was a lot to look at here, and he kind of liked Shawn, though he would never tell his mother that. He picked up a thick stick that had been brought down by a recent storm and practiced swinging it around, sliding into a daydream of being a swashbuckling pirate or a Minecraft hero.

A breeze whispered through the trees and went down his neck, making him shiver. It got cold *fast* here, and he didn't think he liked that so much either. He hugged himself a little, playacting forgotten.

Then he thought he heard voices from somewhere ahead of him. Thinking that perhaps his mom had come into the woods looking for him, he made for the sound, assuming he'd quickly hear her calling his name.

Instead, he heard what sounded like a conversation. Curious now, he followed the noise and found himself at the edge of a small, natural clearing between a bunch of old trees. The temperature had definitely dropped, and a strange smell of incense and iron hung in the air. He clenched his jacket tighter around himself.

There was someone sitting in the middle of the clearing who looked like a big man, and it took a moment for Simon to realize two things: he was sitting on what looked to be a young woman lying on her back, and both of them were wavering, looking almost translucent. He had a knife in his hand and the girl was bleeding out.

Then he looked up and his eyes and mouth grew wide. Simon was sure he heard the strange man scream and then the whole scene vanished before his eyes.

Sunlight beamed down on the clearing, and he shook himself. *I must have imagined it,* he thought. "I must have," he repeated out load.

But there was still the faint smell of blood in the air. And no amount of pinching himself made it go away. It took a brisk breeze whipping through the clearing to carry it away.

"I'm not telling mom," he said, and turned around to make his way back to the house.

The smell of blood suddenly grew stronger, as did the feeling that there was someone behind him. He couldn't help himself – he bolted, still mindful of the tree roots, but he ran until he could see the roof of the house and the smell vanished. Then he dawdled at the edges of the trees, catching his breath, until his mother and little brother came looking for him to go to the beach.

He was happy to go. Anything to get away from that clearing and the ghostly vision of murder.

***

From the air, Prince Rupert looked as though it arched between land and sea like a lazy cougar sprawled on its favorite bed. The bridge connecting the mainland to the Kaien Island where the small port city was found was quite short, but it gave the boys a chance to crane their necks and look for whales, seabirds, and other signs of life.

Harbors branched out from the beach, welcoming small fishing boats and massive cargo ships alike, along with seasonal cruise ships and tankers. The pandemic had slowed the cruise ships down to near nonexistence, and the larger ships were seen less often, but the fishing boats still tacked out every day in the hopes of a catch. Low hills backed the tiny city, and the Coast Mountains loomed over it all, stopped from encroaching by the channel between the island and the mainland. The sky was heavy with clouds, but they had yet to break, painting the city in shades of gray. A bright red coffee shop with an old-fashioned telephone box on the waterfront was a welcome sight.

Other people must have agreed, for the place was humming. A few Indigenous women chatted idly about politics and whose children were squabbling with whom, a coupe of weather-roughened fishers grumbled about the wind, and a few older teenagers loitered at a table, faces buried in their phones. Christopher stayed behind his brother, but Simon looked around in interest. The breeze blew salt air through the open door, mingling with the smell of fresh coffee.

Evelyn didn't particularly need more caffeine, but the pastries looked delicious, and the boys clamoured for pop. Despite the careful spacing of the tables and the masks everyone wore, it was still a touch crowded for her, so she herded the boys back outside once she got their drinks. There they strutted on the docks and yelled at each other to check out boats. Simon stared in amazement at a wooden directional sign that pointed out they were over fifteen hundred kilometers from Vancouver and a mere forty odd kilometres from Alaska.

"We're a long way from home," he said.

Evelyn nodded, feeling a weird lump in her throat. "We are. But this will be a fun summer and we can get a lot out of being here."

"Like see whales," Christopher said. "And mooses. And visiting that funny man, Shawn."

Evelyn laughed a little. "Don't let him hear you call him 'funny'. He might not appreciate it. We can also fix up my uncle's house. Put our own touch on it."

"Are we going to keep it?" Simon asked uncertainly.

Evelyn chewed her lip. "I don't know yet. Probably not. I imagine you're missing Dad and Zan."

Simon kicked at a stray pebble. "I don't think dad misses us."

Fortunately, Christopher was several feet down the boardwalk and hadn't heard that, but Evelyn looked in alarm at Simon. "What do you mean? Of course dad misses you."

Simon gave her a sideways look. "He didn't come see us when we were staying with Zan," he pointed out. "Or visit us at the hospital. And he didn't care that we came here for the whole summer. I think he likes his beer more than he likes us."

Evelyn felt her heart clench and she bent down to look Simon in his sullen, hurt eyes. "Dad is sick," she said quietly. "He has a lot of work to do to get better. But don't doubt for a moment that he loves you. He needs to figure some things out and when he does, he will want to see both of you again."

"*If* he does," Simon muttered. "That house is neat," he said more loudly. "And Shawn seems cool." He felt his own heart give a little clench, but he was still *mad* at his dad for the accident and for just letting them come here without a word. A large part of him hoped that since they were gone, his dad had realized how badly he'd been acting and would come up here and beg for them all to come back, dumping all of his booze into the ocean.

A more cynical part of him, one that had laid seeds down when he'd stumbled over his dad passed out drunk on the couch a year ago, said that it was highly unlikely that would happen soon, if at all.

"I'll be sure to pass that along to Shawn," Evelyn said dryly. She knew Simon didn't want to talk about it anymore, so she let him dash after his brother, but her heart still felt as though it had been stabbed.

Robert is the one who did this to them, not you, she told herself. *He's the one choosing alcohol.*

Of course, she logically knew that it *was* an illness, borne of depression, stress and poor choices. He had to sort himself out before he could even hope to kick the alcohol and *that* would only come with time, outside professional help, and a lot of willpower. But it still hurt to know that Simon thought he counted for less than a can of beer in his father's eyes. She couldn't blame him for thinking it, but she wished he didn't.

The cool salty air went a long way towards letting her keep her tears firmly in check and the boys were delighted with the different gulls and the occasional bald eagle winging low over the ocean. There were plenty of shells to pick up and marvel over. Christopher swore blind he saw an otter, but Simon was openly dubious.

They got groceries at the local store, where Evelyn winced at a higher price tag than she was used to, and then bumped and jostled their way back to the imposing house. The clouds were sinking over the mountains and the air smelled of rain. The first fat drops started falling as they ran bags of food inside and then suddenly turned into a drenching downpour.

"Good thing we left when we did," Evelyn said, leaning a bit against the counter in the kitchen, looking at the rain streaking the window.

"I want to explore more of the house anyway," Simon said. "Come on, Christopher – we haven't seen the basement yet."

Christopher looked skeptical. "Why would we *want* to see the basement?"

"'Cause there's probably more *stuff* down there," Simon said, rolling his eyes. "Come *on*."

"Be careful on those stairs," Evelyn called after them. "They're a bit steep."

The basement door was on the back wall of the kitchen, and it flew open with a bang and closed just as enthusiastically behind her boys. Evelyn winced, hoping they'd turned on the light before getting shut in. The basement was dark with only a couple of small windows to let in the wan, gray light. She unloaded the groceries, feeling tired, and then flicked the coffee machine on.

A yell from downstairs launched her out of her seat and straight down the basement stairs to see Christopher running out of a room across from the bottom of the steps, Simon on his heels. They both nearly careened into her, and it was only by grabbing the stair banister that she was able to keep from being swept off her feet.

"What's *wrong*?" she asked. Christopher's face was white, and he seemed to have lost the power of speech. Simon straightened.

"There's a weird room there with brown stains on the floor like *blood*," he said, his eyes wide. "And a drain in the middle of the floor and sinks on the walls... Mom, why is there a serial killer's room in our house?!"

"You've watched too many horror, and crime shows," Evelyn said. "I'll take a look."

Christopher sat on the stairs, bathed in the light seeping from the kitchen. Simon positioned himself between his brother and his mother, and Evelyn made her way to the door they'd left hanging open.

She could see at a glance why the room had spooked her boys. It wasn't very large, but oddly wide, with stainless steel paneling the walls, and strong counters lining two walls while the other wall had deep sinks and shelves. The door had let her in on one corner of it, opening out to give the most amount of space possible.

There were a few extremely dusty jars on the shelves and Evelyn decided she could wait until it was sunny to see what was inside of them. There was a closed drain in the middle of the floor and, hanging from the ceiling above, a very thick and slightly rusty hook. Brown splotches stained the floor around the drain and a few ancient splatters could be seen near the counters and sinks. The lightbulb was flickering fitfully, about to die, and more bars were hanging from the ceiling, though they didn't have any hooks on them.

She came back out and hugged Simon and Christopher.

"It's a butchering room," she said. "Uncle Jason used to hunt with the locals, and they'd do some of the butchering here at the house. The hook is where they probably hung the carcass of whatever they killed so they could start processing it, and then they'd cut it all up and freeze the meat. Shawn told me this room was down here, but it probably hasn't been used in a while. You boys certainly don't need to go in there for anything."

"I'm going back upstairs," Christopher declared, but Simon lingered.

"Are you going to tear that room out," he asked.

"I don't think it can just be torn out," she said. "But maybe it can be changed into something else. Or maybe it could be cleaned and used by the locals again. A lot of people hunt around here."

Simon chewed his lip. "It's creepy."

"There's nothing to worry about," Evelyn said firmly. "And think: that room was used to help people get enough meat to eat all winter. That's important."

"I guess," he said, wrinkling his nose and following his brother upstairs.

Evelyn paused. She'd closed the door of the butcher room, but she wondered if she should find a way to lock it. Despite how useful she knew it had been, it was giving her the creeps too, and she contemplated the possibility of completely tearing it out or cementing it up. She started to follow her boys and was part way up the stairs when something banged behind her. She whipped around, but the basement was still.

"Imagination is getting away from me," she muttered and shut the basement door firmly behind her.

Chapter Five

The rain stopped by mid-afternoon and the boys charged outside to chase each other in the wet grass. Evelyn half watched them from the window, but she was more interested in finishing her unpacking. She could certainly hear them – they yelled and screamed like wild animals. When they quieted, she looked up to see that they were circling the greenhouse. She shrugged and returned to her things. It was likely locked anyway.

Christopher peered through the grubby glass and at first, didn't see much to interest him. There were a couple of bags of dirt, some long, raised planter boxes, and a small pile of garden pots. A few tools hung from the corners.

But then a shadow seemed to cross his eyes and for a moment he was sure he saw a man hunched over in one of the corners.

"Simon!" he called, trying to keep the man in sight and hoping he wouldn't be noticed in turn. The silhouette kept fading in and out sight, making it hard to track. "There's something living in our greenhouse!"

Simon scoffed, but he came over anyway and looked over his brother's head.

The man looked up and they saw he had golden eyes and shaggy dark hair. For a moment, both boys were sure they saw something that looked as though it was coming out of his *back*, through his jacket.

"I'm getting mom," Simon said immediately. "Stay outside. And if that guy moves towards you, run!"

Christopher moved back a little anyway, but the man was wavering and, just as the back door banged open and Evelyn came running out, he vanished.

"Are you alright?" she asked Christopher. He shrugged. She looked over his head and then crossed her arms. "Are you boys playing a game?"

"What do you mean?" Simon demanded. He looked through the glass as well and then glared at Christopher. "Where'd he go?"

"I dunno," Christopher said, stung at the feeling that this was all somehow his fault. "He disappeared."

Evelyn huffed a sigh. "I'll check it out," she said. "But don't lock the door behind me."

"We wouldn't do that," Simon said. "Shouldn't we call the police?"

"People sometimes need a place to stay," Evelyn said and opened the door. She walked around the inside, but all she saw was a few half-empty bags of fertilizer that she supposed *might* look like a person if the boys were feeling particularly imaginative.

"There's no one here," Evelyn said. "You boys are letting your imaginations get away from you."

Christopher's face fell into a frown and Simon crossed his arms over his chest as their mother walked back into the house.

"There was *so* someone there," Christopher sulked.

Simon shook his head. "Whoever – whatever – it was, it's gone now."

The two boys exchanged mutinous looks and went back to playing, overseen by an unnoticed raven in a nearby tree.

***

The paperwork wasn't enough to keep Shawn's mind off the weird house and the family of three now staying in it for the summer.

After Jason passed away in his own house, some of the elders had done a smudging at the request of Shawn's aunt who had never felt very comfortable there. But even after it was done, it was hard to find anyone who would go near the old house. When his aunt returned from the smudging, she was shaken and confused for days afterwards and even now wouldn't speak of the experience.

Something tainted had sunk into the very bones of the house, seeping like toxic waste.

Try telling someone from Vancouver about weird feelings in an old house and see how far you get, though. Even here, there was no one who believed him about the missing tourists and teenagers being connected to the house somehow, and they all knew him and the cases.

"Shawn," his father said curtly, and he snapped himself back to reality. Then he felt guilty. This case was critical to several of the fishermen in the area and would strike a blow against the massive fisheries trying to get a foothold in the area. He really had to pay attention, or at least one auntie would fetch him a blow upside the head, and he'd deserve it.

But as the interviews continued, his mind went back to the house in the hills. His father eventually gave up on his son being much use; after lunch, he kicked him out with a snort of annoyance and a firm glare which promised a verbal butt-kick if Shawn came anywhere near him for the rest of the day without his head in the game.

"Maybe being a lawyer isn't my calling after all," he said aloud, watching the gray clouds scuttle across the sky.

Sadly, ghost hunting wasn't a profession at all, so that avenue was closed to him before it even began. But there was something strange about that house and while he wasn't sure how to tell Evelyn about it without sounding like an idiot, he knew that *something* would need to be done.

The beach was busy, despite the impending rain. There had been rumors for several days of a shooting star over the ocean and ever since then, people had been drifting in and out, looking for meteorites. No one had found anything like that, but there were always shells and nice rocks to add to various collections. Seagulls wheeled overhead, occasionally flitting down to grab someone's lunch, eliciting curses. Shawn grinned a little as he watched the birds annoy people. Everyone else thought them dirty and obnoxious, but Shawn always liked them.

One of the elders had drifted closer to him. Her dark eyes were nearly lost in wrinkles and her steel gray hair was carefully braided and bounded at the nape of her neck. She was wearing a good raincoat to ward off the weather and was holding a bag of groceries. She hummed to herself as she watched the beachgoers.

"*Ama gawdi suulgyaxs,*" he said respectfully, and she grinned up at him, revealing at least three missing teeth.

"It's been an age since I heard those words coming out of a young man's mouth," she said, smirking a little. "I thought you were on your Instagrams all the time, with no time to learn any of the old ways."

"I try to put something in my head every so often," Shawn joked. She tapped him with her walking cane.

"Then you should be listening to your *Łagyigyet,*" she said, and Shawn made a mental note to look up the word. "Young folk these days don't do that enough. Solve all that frowning, yeah?" She chortled to herself. "Or add to it."

"I'll do my best," Shawn said as a compromise since he wasn't sure what she was talking about. She tapped him with her cane again and then headed for the bus stop to return her to one of the reserves, or at least close enough that a family member could pick her up.

It had felt like an odd conversation, but at least it had given him some distraction from his thoughts.

***

Evelyn woke up to another gray day and a feeling that summers here would be nothing like most summers on the southern coast. To be fair, she had been warned that this part of British Columbia was soggy, but she really hoped it wouldn't rain *all* summer, or else the boys were going to run wild and destroy the house.

At least they didn't seem to mind exploring for now, so they wouldn't be shredding things just yet. And they still had their books and video games.

The boys were already occupied with figuring out the television in the living room. Sadly, it wasn't offering much in the way of cable, but at least Simon could get their Switch connected. Evelyn braced herself and went outside to look at the greenhouse more closely. She'd never taken the time to learn how to grow anything, but some part of her had always thought that growing flowers at least would be relaxing, and the building had been weighing on her mind since the day before.

The greenhouse had looked in reasonably good shape when she'd gone in to investigate the boys' claims that there was a person in it. Although whoever had trimmed the lawn had yet to make an appearance, whoever once handled the greenhouse left the building in good shape. It was about the size of the living room and lined with pots, upraised planter boxes and several tools and bags of dirt. There was a slightly crude system of water hoses lining the walls, though they weren't connected to anything. When she looked outside, she saw a tap drilled into the ground and well insulated against frost and ice.

The glass was filthy, so the gray light was even dingier, but it was just dirt and water stains so it would be easy to clean. The pots and planter boxes looked to be in good shape, with a just a bit of damage on corners.

She did have the weird feeling that she wasn't alone, though. It was like when Simon was little, and he'd quietly follow her around to see what she was doing. She'd get the itchy feeling up her neck and then whip around to see him grinning at her, hoping for a cookie. This time though, when she turned, she saw nothing but the occasional glimpse of her own reflection.

"Picking up on what the kids were imagining," she muttered. It was easy to think that the pile of fertilizer bags was a man slouched over on himself, but of course there was no one else with her.

"Just too used to living in places with lots of people everywhere," she firmly told herself. "It'll take time to get used to the solitude out here." She redirected her attention to the greenhouse, but the feeling of being watched remained.

When the greenhouse door opened and a throat cleared behind her, she jumped a foot in the air and whipped around with a small shovel clutched in her hands.

The man in the doorway raised an eyebrow.

"I'm sorry," he said, and her heart hammered.

"Who are you?!" she demanded.

He blinked and for a moment, she thought that he was somehow confused by the question. "Kal," he said. "I work – worked? – as the gardener here. I'm sorry for not coming sooner. I was held up in Terrace with family."

"Oh," she said, willing her body to *calm down.* "I'm Evelyn."

"I thought so," he said. "I was aware of your uncle's will."

He stepped a little closer and held out a hand for her to shake. His leather jacket creaked a little, glistening with the first rain drops.

Evelyn hastily dropped the shovel and shook his hand. A spark of electricity jumped between them, and she dropped his hand in surprise.

"Sorry," he said, shaking his fingers. "I do that to everyone. Some people are just more… charged than others, or so I've heard. I can't wear a watch, and I don't bother carrying a phone."

She tilted her head at him. He didn't *look* much like a gardener. He had almost black hair that was a bit long and what Zan would call *chiseled* features. He was taller than her by nearly a foot and while his jeans were beat up, his leather jacket looked nearly pristine. Strangest of all were his eyes – they caught the meagre light and flashed them with gold for a moment before settling on a strange green-brown color. *Hazel, I think that's sometimes called.* He had a beat-up motorcycle helmet swinging from one hand.

"I thought I should at least give you the chance to let me go with some dignity," he said. "Or decide to keep me on. Either way." He sounded strangely unbothered at the possibility that he might be out a job, but perhaps he had another one lined up or this one hadn't meant a lot to him.

"I don't know much about taking care of a yard or a greenhouse like this," she said. "Or those roses out front. But I don't even know if I'm going to keep this house. The next owners are the people you'll really have to talk to after the summer."

He shrugged. "Then I'll do that. But in the meantime?"

"You might as well stay on," she said, a little surprised at herself. "Like I said, you know more about all of this than I do."

"True," he said. "I'd shake on it, but you don't need to get zapped again. Your uncle was paying me a flat fee – five hundred a week – to come in and do the groundwork and grow vegetables in the greenhouse. Sound fair?"

"I guess," she said, a little flustered. It wouldn't do much to her fattened bank account for only two months anyway. "Thank you."

He shrugged again. "I look forward to working with you, Evelyn." He looked over her head. "I should tidy up in here and get things growing again. Your uncle shooed me out when he was dying and then the house was in limbo for a while.... It needs some work."

"Yeah," Evelyn said, sliding around him. "I'll leave you to it."

And she did just that, letting him start heaving bags of fertilizer into the planter boxes and get he water system hooked up again.

She supposed that were this a rom-com, her heart would be fluttering. Objectively, he was handsome, (*"Gorgeous,"* sighed Zan's voice in her head), but if anything, her heart was still racing in alarm, not lust.

"Gorgeous like a marble statue," she muttered back at Zan's ghost while she trudged back to the house. "A slightly creepy marble statue. Besides, if I kissed him, he might electrocute me into a coma."

It was a weird condition to have, but it might explain why he was working around plants instead of people. She tossed a look over her shoulder, but he was doing nothing sinister unless one had tender feelings towards weeds.

***

The day, which had started gray and dripping rain, was turning out to be rather nice for a quick road trip, and a new little bakery had bravely opened its doors in Port Edward. It was highly unlikely that Evelyn knew about it, so Shawn had a built-in excuse to see her in the form of fresh baked treats, and ready reason to scratch the itch that the old house had planted in his imagination.

He didn't really want to admit that to himself, but he did want to see more of the house for himself. When his aunts had conducted a smudging after Jason died, he'd stayed well away. But something drew him back now, and it wasn't just the woman staying there.

"Listen to your ancestors," he told his rearview mirror. He'd looked up the strange word on his phone. "Well, since I was dreaming of my grandmother last night, that's as close as I'm going to get."

It hadn't been *much* of a dream, just her looking worried and patting his head like she did when he was a child, but it was something. He could hear his old professors muttering about patterns and foolishness, but it was easy to put that all out of his head in favor of fresh fry bread and croissants. He absently wondered if the boys had ever eaten fry bread before and what they would make of it. Then he turned his jeep on the road south.

The sun shone overhead, but the trees loomed, creating stripes of shadow on the pavement. It was getting on in the morning, so there was no wildlife larger than birds and squirrels near the road, but he kept an eye out anyway. One never knew when a bear would decide to trundle out of the brush to start munching on dandelions. Moose had little respect for the rules of the road. In a confrontation between a moose and just about anything smaller than a semi, the moose won.

The drive to the old house wasn't long, but the rough, narrow road up always felt like it took more than its fair share of the time, winding its way through the hills until it found a flat place. He pulled up alongside Evelyn's SUV, relieved that she was actually there, and hopped out.

The sun didn't exactly do the exterior of the house any favours. The paint was peeling, and the yard was starting to get overgrown. As he took it in, Evelyn appeared around the corner and stared at him.

"Shawn, what are you doing here?" she asked, walking over to him.

"Brought you some treats from a new bakery in Port Edward," he said, holding out the pair of boxes. "It just opened, and the owners are nervous about it. I figured you wouldn't have heard about it yet."

She looked uncertain, but she took the boxes from him.

"It's a housewarming gift, I guess," he said, trying again. "Fry bread and croissants. Figured I'd get you the best form both sides of the country."

She smiled at that, and the boys came running out the door, having seen the jeep pull up. Christopher hid a little behind Evelyn, but Simon faced the taller man head-on.

"I've been trying to say good morning like you do, but it comes out wrong," he complained, and Shawn laughed.

"It took me a while to get it right too," he said. "Start small."

Simon didn't look happy about that advice, but he nodded.

"Take these inside for me?" Evelyn asked and the boys darted away with the boxes. She had her doubts they would make it far unopened. She stepped back a pace from Shawn, still looking vaguely suspicious.

"Thank you," she said. "Is there anything else?"

Shawn tilted his head at her. "Not in particular," he admitted. "I was kinda curious to see the house again is all. I haven't been here before now."

"My uncle was an important part of the community, wasn't he?" Evelyn asked.

"Sort of," Shawn said, lounging against his jeep. The sun felt good on his skin, and it was a rare occurrence on the coast. "He went hunting a lot and would share his supplies and his space so that more work could be done in the fall for the winter. He wasn't made an official part of any clan, but a lot of people liked him, my dad included."

"Clan?"

Shawn waved a hand. "Eagle, Killer Whale, Raven, and Wolf." He grinned and mimed shaking her hand. "Shawn Myers, Raven Clan. Well, once in a while, white people get kind of 'adopted' in, but he never did. Some of the elders discussed it, but he always talked them out of it. He never felt as though he deserved it."

Evelyn crossed her arms over her stomach. "Did you know him?"

Shawn puffed out a breath. "Not really," he said. "I went to university out east for my law degree and then I worked out there for a year or two before coming back here to help dad. I've only been home for a year and our paths never really crossed. My dad was friends with him, though, and Jason's death hit him pretty hard. That's why he wanted to make sure the will was all done properly. You must have been close to him."

"When I was young, I was," she said. "Sort of. He wrote a lot of letters. He came for my wedding and Simon's birth, but he didn't stay long. Mom drove him away – she hates him and won't talk about why." The phone call where Evelyn had told her mother about the house had ended in dire warnings that Evelyn shouldn't go anywhere near it, but no explanation as to why.

"He didn't come for Christopher's birth." She frowned. "If you're asking why he passed the house down to me, I can't answer you. I thought it would have gone to... well, someone else. Though I don't know who – he never married or had children. Maybe it should have gone to a couple of cousins or something." She shrugged.

"I guess he left a few things to other people, but I doubt anyone else was thrilled when they heard none of them got the house," Shawn said wryly. "Maybe he thought you'd fit in around here better than anyone else in his family."

"I can't imagine why he thought *I* would," Evelyn sighed. "But it's been nice to be away from the city. I'm sure I won't be saying that in a couple of weeks."

Shawn stretched against his jeep. "You get used to it or you go nuts," he said cheerfully, and she gave him a dark look which he laughed at. "Is there anything you need? I can at least direct you to good places to find stuff."

"Just things like paint," Evelyn said. "I don't really know a lot about home repair, but it would be good to update things a little."

"Home Hardware in Prince Rupert," Shawn said. "It's at the mall." He suddenly looked sheepish. "All right, it's not *much* of a mall compared to what you're probably used to, but they should have what you need."

"We haven't really explored Prince Rupert yet," she said. "I took the boys the other day to get some groceries, but I want to spend more time there. Hopefully on a day that stays sunny."

"The Timmies is close to there too," Shawn said.

Coffee, donuts, and some proper tools did sound like a good idea to Evelyn, though if she was being honest with herself, simply getting away from the house sounded even better. She wasn't about to say anything about her unease to Shawn though. He'd probably think she was being silly.

Shawn seemed to sense her awkwardness. He nodded farewell to her and got back in his vehicle. She dropped her arms to her side and watched him slowly back out and drive away, feeling a weird pang. She felt bad that he had come out just to be practically rebuffed at the driveway, but at the same time, she didn't want him hanging around and couldn't figure out why. She sighed and made her way back into a house that was starting to feel more alien to her rather than less.

Shawn did drive away, but only a short distance and then he hopped out and stared around at the woods. He was still close enough that he could see the roof of the house in snatched glances through the tree boughs, but that wasn't what was holding his attention. There was the feeling of something watching him, waiting for him to leave. *Pushing* him to leave.

I'm a trained lawyer, not a superstitious kid, he scolded himself, but the presence didn't seem impressed. It only loomed more heavily, making him think that leaving was a very good idea. Thoughts that he'd left his door unlocked floated through his mind, all the work he had to do and a fast-approaching deadline...

He had almost climbed back into his jeep without realizing it, and then turned to face the trees.

"Cute," he said. "Really cute. And then what? Gonna keep lurking in the woods until someone else comes along you don't like? It won't work, whatever you are."

This time, he was absolutely *certain* that there was a moose nearby and if he moved from the jeep, it would charge him. He could hear the brush rattling and even saw a large shape browsing on the leaves. But he gritted his teeth, gripped the top of the door until the edge from the rolled down window made a deep impression int the palm of his hand and took several steadying breaths. There was no odor of wild animal and that told him he was imagining things – or something was *making* him imagine things.

Does Sasquatch do stuff like that? He'd never heard of lore like that and he hadn't made a study of the tales of the northwest, aside from what his *nsT'its* used to tell him. He was starting to regret that hole in his education and made a mental note to ask his father or one of the aunts or elders about it.

There really was nothing he could do about it now, so with a final warning glare at the trees, he got into his jeep, making it clear he was doing so under *his* power, and drove away. The feeling didn't abate until he was almost to the main road, when it abruptly vanished and cold sweat sprang on his brow.

"Something to do with Evelyn and the boys being there?" They hadn't struck him as the types to bring anything strange with them, but he could be wrong.

It was something to ask his family about and maybe some of the elders. And since Evelyn was unlikely to believe him without any proof, there was little sense in worrying her about it. She didn't trust him as it was without her thinking he was crazy.

Chapter Six

Evelyn wanted to go into town for the afternoon, but the boys were violently opposed to the idea. Stuffed full of fry bread, they were intent on yelling at each other, threatening mayhem, and sulking. Evelyn was in no mood to drag them around shopping, so she banished them to their rooms to work out their moods by themselves while she made more coffee and tried not to brood.

It should have been a lovely day to go out, but the sunshine seemed weirdly muted. She wondered if she was simply feeling lonely and homesick, so she picked up the phone to call Zan.

"You've reached your local Goddess of Health and Wellbeing, Zan Corshire. Leave your prayers at the beep and I will get back to you as soon as I can. Love you!"

Evelyn left her usual message – a derisive snort at her friend's message – and then hung up, feeling dispirited. Zan was probably out hiking or eating a late brunch or perhaps even at work. The thought of it only made her feel worse, adding to her suspicion that she was homesick.

"Well," she said to her cup. "I can't just wait around for someone to drag me out of it."

It was a very Zan thing to say and it made her feel a bit better. She tucked her phone in her pocket, in case the Goddess of Health and Wellbeing deigned to call her back, and then went back outside to pound some more planks into the slightly rickety back porch she was putting back together.

She wasn't much of a handyman, but there was something soothing about laying boards out, making sure they were even and pounding nails into them to hold them into the older frame. It was almost meditative and she vaguely thought she should bring it to Zan's attention for one of her weekend classes.

Then her neck started itching. Figuring it was a mosquito, she swatted it, but there was nothing there. She shifted out of the sun a little, but the crawling feeling only intensified. She looked up and around to see a strange, dark figure standing in the middle of the yard between the house and greenhouse. The sunlight was cascading around it, but the figure itself was completely dark.

Evelyn scrambled to her feet and held the hammer as though it were a much larger weapon, brandishing it between herself and the figure. The thing didn't move towards her, though it seemed to waver a little in the sunshine. Then it reached out towards her and she screamed.

Her scream did a far better job of dissuading the figure than her hammer did. It shattered as though the soundwaves from her voice had destroyed it, leaving an empty yard in its wake.

Simon's head popped out of the window above her. "Mom! Are you okay?"

Evelyn turned. "I'm fine," she said, managing to keep her voice steady. "I just thought I saw something, and I was so busy working that it startled me. Don't worry about it."

Simon looked a little suspicious, but he took her word for it and vanished back into his room. She sagged a little, holding her knees.

It had been so fleeting and unexpected that a large part of her wondered if she'd simply imagined the whole thing, a phantom born of weariness and sorrow. That's what made *sense* after all – just a figment of her imagination, provoked by the boys talking about seeing a man in the greenhouse and meeting the strange gardener.

But she still felt a chill resting on her spine and a deep certainty that she'd seen *something*.

The back porch could wait. She went back inside and firmly shut the door on all beings, real or imagined.

***

For a few nights after finding the butcher room, Simon dreamed of the woods.

He was standing at the window, looking beyond the greenhouse, and looking at the fir trees which, because it was a dream, were all outlined in silver, letting him clearly see the path back to the strange clearing. This time, though, there was no man murdering a woman. Instead, it was just a man who looked a little like his mom, with the same gray eyes. He wasn't wearing a shirt and had something dark and sticky-looking smeared across his chest. He was holding a knife up to the moon.

Then there was a weird odour, dry and acrid, and the strange man's face twisted in fury. He lunged out towards the house and vanished.

Simon always woke up at that point.

This time, it was a half-moon shining through his window, and he padded over to it to look outside. The trees were dark blotches against the sky, and he couldn't see much beyond the greenhouse, which only had one corner visible due to the light from the back porch. The pale white light couldn't go beyond a certain point before it transitioned to darkness. If he craned his neck, he could look up and see the stars like scattered diamonds.

It really was nothing like home here. He shivered a little.

Mom might be right about the horror shows and books. He'd read a good book over the past few days, but maybe it had gotten into his dreams, leading him to where he was now.

He really was trying to tell himself that everything – the weird man in the greenhouse, the strange feeling in the basement, the vision in the woods – was all in his imagination, or had some other reasonable explanation, but he couldn't think what it would be. He knew he should tell his mother about it all too, but he wasn't sure how, and she hadn't believed him about the thing in the greenhouse.

And forget telling his dad at all.

He wished Zan was around. Or Shawn. He might know something about weird things in the woods. He was Indigenous after all, it stood to reason that he'd know about weird ghostly things in the forest and in his greenhouse.

Christopher was moving restlessly in his own room across the hall; Simon could hear him tossing and turning. He frowned at his faint reflection in the window. His brother wasn't taking this well either. He was homesick, and the man in the greenhouse and the butcher room had scared him a lot more than it had Simon. At least he didn't seem interested in going in the woods.

The wind moved through the trees, causing them to ripple as though they were saying hello to him.

He yanked the curtains closed. "Nope," he said aloud. "There's probably bears out there now. And maybe wolves." He turned his back, got into bed, and pulled the covers over his head.

But the smell of the trees seemed to seep through the window, making him think of wild things and running on pine needles.

And a man who wasn't his dad, but he *felt* like he wanted to be a good dad.

***

In Port Edward, Shawn's eyes were aching for a sleep that was proving elusive. And even when he did finally drop off, he never stayed there long before a dream, or a nightmare, chased him back out again.

He gave up on the whole thing as a bad idea at three in the morning and went to the small kitchen to brew some tea.

He flicked on the light, expecting to see the usual small room with battered tile flooring, off-white coloured appliances, and a scratched up little table, but instead his attention was drawn to a thin woman half slumped over his table, her fingers wrapped around a bottle of Corona, the fumes of beer wafting around her. He quickly saw how she'd gotten in – the key to his house was lying under her other hand.

He groaned a little, rubbed his eyes in the vague hope that she'd disappear, and when she didn't, he intentionally banged into the table with his hip, jarring her from her stupor and sloshing her beer.

"Oh," she said, looking blearily up through her lank black hair. "Hi, cuz."

"Hi, *cousin*," he said, putting an annoyed emphasis on the relation. "What are you doing here?"

She looked at the bottle and then up at him and shrugged. "Dunno," she said, sounding mystified as well. "I thought I was home."

"Way off course this time, Lori," he said. "You live a few blocks away. What, did your ride just dump you off at the first familiar place?" He was going to *murder* Trevor.

She shook her head. "Didn't have a ride."

He banged the kettle, waking her up further and drawing her gaze to something that *wasn't* alcoholic. She looked hopefully at the kettle and then back at him. "Maybe it will help you sober up," he commented, though he wasn't holding out hope.

With that goal in mind, he swapped her half full bottle of *his* beer, he noted with exasperation, for a plate of cookies, and turned the kettle on, dumping the beer into the sink. She looked despondent at that, but she knew better than to say anything.

"What do you mean, you didn't have a ride?" he said, getting back to the topic at hand. "Who were you with?"

"Bunch of people," she said, resting her head on her arms. "I dunno. Didn't stay with me."

"Well, where's Trevor?" *That ass.*

"Don't care," she said, finally a glint of something other than morose in her deep brown eyes. "Jackass can go jump in the ocean."

"Trouble in paradise?" he asked blandly, borrowing one of his old roommate's favourite phrases. She glared at him.

"He's a *tool*," she said. "I'm over with losers."

Uh huh, he thought, but didn't say anything. Instead, he nudged the plate closer to her, trying to encourage her to pad her stomach with something other than beer. She grabbed one of the cookies, but only crumbled it a little in her hand.

"I dumped him," she said firmly and stuffed the cookie in her mouth to end any chance at further questions.

Shawn sighed and put tea bags into thick mugs. His grandmother would murder him if she were still alive and knew about it, but what she didn't know wouldn't earn him a rap upside the head for using *colonizer* tea. He was fine with using the loose leaf she had always used, but not at three in the morning when his cousin was half passed out on his table. There was a time and place for everything, and this was the time for tea bags. He vaguely wondered if they were stale, but his cousin probably wouldn't even notice, and he just wanted something warm to hold.

At least she did drink half the mug off as soon as he gave it to her, spluttering at the scalding liquid on her tongue.

"Thank you," she said stiffly, and he sighed again. "Do you mind if I stay here?"

"Little late to be asking now," he snorted.

"I couldn't *wake you up*," she said, rolling her eyes as though *he* was the idiot who was half-wasted in someone else's house.

He'd always vaguely admired her ability to deflect what she should be feeling onto the nearest person. It also annoyed the hell out of him.

"Might as well. You're already here, drinking my beer."

"You stock crap, by the way."

"Beggars can't be choosers," he retorted. "It's not like I was expecting to be entertaining my cousin of such discerning tastes."

She grinned at him and then put her head back into her arms. "Except when it comes to guys," came her muffled voice. "No taste there."

"Except for whoever enables you best."

He didn't need to see her face to know that she was glaring at him, but he was sleep deprived and in no mood to coddle his wayward younger cousin who probably wouldn't even remember most of this conversation come noon.

"You're mean," she said.

"Yup," he said. "Hasn't stopped you form drinking my beer and sleeping on my table."

"I didn't know where the guest room was. Big fancy lawyer you are."

He snorted, glancing around his small kitchen. "You're fine with me being a big fancy lawyer when it suits you," he sighed. "Finish your tea and I'll show you to a bed instead of the table."

"Okay," she said and swallowed the rest of her tea. Then he half carried, half dragged her to the spare room on the main floor of his house and practically dropped her on the bed. Feeling the tug of familial guilt for not being nicer to her, he yanked off her shoes and tucked her in properly. She was asleep seconds later and he rubbed his face as he closed the door behind him.

Lori hit the bottom again.

It was a recurring pattern, not just for her, but for many in his family. Lori had grown up with alcohol a constant companion in her house, the threat of her and her siblings being taken away a regular occurrence, and the shrugging off of anything resembling an education. She had managed to make her way to adulthood largely due to stubbornness, Shawn watching out for her, and some luck, but as she partied her way through her teens and early twenties, he'd been forced to let go of the dream that she would completely break free and make something better of herself.

At some point, he might have to cut her loose entirely, but he wasn't ready for that. The thought of her being homeless made him feel awful; the place she lived in now was less a house than a half-wrecked trailer that was also home to mice and spiders. Once in a while, she would end up at his door and he always let her in to shower, eat a few square meals, and spend a day sober before she got dragged back into the alcoholic abyss by any number of friends and other family members.

Sometimes I wonder why that wasn't me too, he thought with a hefty twinge of guilt. They were family after all and had all been neighbors growing up. Why did she fall into alcoholism and abuse, while he'd finished his schooling and secured work? It didn't seem right or fair.

"You're not doing this again," he muttered aloud. "Lori made her choices. Dad tried to help her too."

That was why he *didn't* like to see her too often. He always felt guilty and, if her parents or older siblings were around, they *made* him feel like garbage too.

"*Apple...*" His cousins used to taunt him with that, especially when he brought home good grades and whispers of scholarships to come. *"What do you want to go out east for? Nothing out there for you. You think those white kids will give a shit how smart you think you are? Nah, you'll be tossed out. Or they'll make you forget your roots."* This was usually followed by a cousin punching him, another one jabbing at him with a bottle, and him leaving.

He ground his fists into his eyes, reminding himself of the *hours, years* of work he'd put into his degree, the homesickness, the fights, and yes, the derision he had faced even from the professors who assumed he would leave midway through the first year.

And how proud dad was.

Most of his family in Port Edward and Prince Rupert hadn't been very supportive, but his dad was proud. And his grandmother would have been, if she'd lived long enough to see him graduate. She had always said that the best way to fight poison was with knowledge of the poison, so the best way to fight back against colonialism and its impact was to *understand* it, work the system until it was soft in your hands, and then strike.

He wasn't going to let Lori's reappearance shake him.

Fortified by the voice of his grandmother in his ear and the memory of his dad beaming ear to ear when he graduated, he straightened up and returned to his bed. If he was dealing with a weird house on one side and Lori on the other, he would need all the rest he could.

Chapter Seven

When Shawn got up late the next morning, it was to Lori nursing a cup of coffee. She had red eyes and still looked exhausted, but she was more or less sober.

"Hey cuz," he said. "How are you?"

"Ugh," she answered.

"Sounds right," he said, hauling out the toaster. "Cure for that is grease. Bacon? Toast?"

"Fry bread?" she asked hopefully, and he gave her a rueful look.

"I could, but I don't know how good it will be."

She shrugged and he sighed, but he set to his task with a will. It wouldn't be inedible by a long shot, but there were people far better at making fry bread than he was, and she would likely remind him of that fact.

To his surprise, when he brought her a plate with some jarred salmon on the side, she ate the whole thing, looking cheerful. He shrugged, not about to question his cousin's sudden friendliness, and ate a piece himself.

"Are you going to finish sleeping it off here?" he asked. "I have to go to work, is all."

She puffed out a sigh and looked like she was going to say something scathing, but it died in her mouth. "Thank you," she said instead. "For putting up with me like this. I shouldn't have just dumped on you, eh?"

"It's not the first time, and it probably won't be the last," he said. "Just bad timing if you wanted me around today. Dad needs my help this morning, and I have some loose ends of my own to tie up."

She waved a hand. "It's fine," she said. "You're probably right about me sleeping some more. I won't be in your hair for long. I haven't been home in a few days. I should check on it."

He frowned at her. "Where *have* you been, then?"

"Around," she said vaguely, put another piece of fry bread in her mouth to ward off further questions, and then wandered away. He sighed and got ready for work.

There was no point in grilling her further. She would talk, or not, under her own volition. He was leaning towards her *not* talking. She'd never opened up to him before, despite regularly crashing in his spare room, but he had been surprised before. He got ready to go to Prince Rupert slowly, in the hopes of encouraging her to speak up, but the guest room door remained resolutely closed, and he knew that when he would come home later, she'd be gone.

"You can't save everyone," his dad said sadly after his young cousin had been found dead of an overdose. They'd been

close and Shawn had talked him off the ledge many times, but this time he had been too late. "Some people are only with us a short time before they are called away."

He thought to go into law in the hopes of preventing harm to others, but sometimes he wondered if he went the wrong way somewhere. No one he wanted to help wanted to talk to him since he'd returned from Ontario, degree in hand.

Too late for regrets now.

There was some paperwork to be done but, as noon approached, Shawn found himself staring south and then, without really considering it, he resolutely stood up and grabbed his jacket and keys.

"Going to check on the house and Evelyn," he said. "And bring her the final paperwork and the card of the realtor who can take it off her hands if she wants to sell. I'll take some pictures of those trawlers for you too."

"You mean Grace?" his dad said wryly.

"She'd be mad as hell at me if I didn't give her a chance at the house," Shawn laughed. "So, I figure I'd better give Evelyn her contact information."

His dad frowned, the wrinkles around his mouth and on his forehead deepening. "Is everything going all right there?"

"I think so," Shawn said. "Why?"

His father shook his head a little. "I don't know. Every time I think of going to pay my respects, I get a bad feeling about it.

I really should have gone when Evelyn first arrived, but this case ate my time, and I don't know... Bad feeling."

Shawn shrugged. "It seems fine to me," he said, though a shivery feeling crawled up his spine at the thought of seeing the house again. "Just battered. I guess Jason hadn't been working on it much."

"Probably couldn't," his father said. "When his health went, it went *fast*. Be careful out there."

Shawn gave him a surprised look. "Middle of summer, the bears and moose won't bother with me."

"Like I said, a bad feeling."

"I'll be careful."

His dad patted his shoulder. "And Liz said Lori was missing. Have you seen her?"

"She slept at my place last night and said she'd be going back to the trailer today. She didn't tell me where she's been."

His dad sighed. "How did she look?"

"Tired, drunk, and too thin. Typical Lori."

"I'll let Liz know her wayward daughter is home," he said. "She can take things up from there if she wants to."

They both knew Liz wouldn't.

***

For all the faults of the house and the isolation, Evelyn did like the mornings. Everything else was shabby or inconvenient, but the sun coming up over the trees and mountains had yet to fail to cheer her up. She would take her coffee to the back porch and watch the light as it pooled into the greenhouse and then crept over the house as though waiting for an invitation.

It also banished any uneasy feelings that the night had left her with. And the night often left her with those. She wasn't used to the quiet yet and would wake up with the sound of her heart in her ears.

"Three AM regrets," she said aloud. The hour where she wondered if divorcing Robert, not looking for work yet, and coming up here to stay in the middle of nowhere for the summer had been the most terrible ideas of her life. These thoughts were always in her mother's voice, which made it doubly worse. And there was no Zan to run interference now. She could call, but it wasn't the same, and Zan wouldn't thank her for the three-in-the-morning wake-up call.

By day, she knew she *had* to leave Robert, that she wasn't ready to look for a new job, and that coming here was a good idea, isolation aside.

It was still hard to tell herself that at three in the morning.

Kal was already in the greenhouse, hauling out dirt and tools. He seemed to like early mornings as well, preferring to be gone by noon. She was getting used to the slightly anemic rumble of his ancient motorcycle as it came to and from the house. She idly watched him line up his tools and start to pull out the weeds that were sneaking close to the greenhouse.

She thought about wishing him a good morning, but she also felt oddly shy.

And then there was Simon. He'd been spending a lot of time simply staring at the forest around them. She'd tried to ask him about it, but he'd only shrugged. It was hard to explain to Christopher why his brother was acting the way he was, but she was chalking it up to the fact that he was rocketing his way to being a teenager and all the angst that held.

He didn't seem sad or angry anyway, just distant. She'd tried to figure out if he was homesick, but every time she broached the subject, she hit a wall of indifference and bounced off.

"I do wish you were here, Zan," she murmured. "You'd be able to figure out what's going through his head.

Logically, homesickness and missing his dad made the most sense. It didn't make her feel any better, but it made sense.

She shook it off as best she could. Today, she planned to paint some of the rooms that weren't being used and work her way around to the other rooms. It had been a while since she had last taken up a roller and brush; not since Christopher's nursery, and she remembered it being a lot of work, but also something of an artistic release and oddly satisfying. She was looking forward to doing it again, with the buckets of paint to prove it. The walls of the spare room were stripped and now they just awaited their new coats.

By noon, she had managed to get most of the smallest bedroom finished with one coat and was thinking of taking a rest when she heard a familiar crunching noise coming from outside: Shawn's jeep.

That was another thing keeping her awake at three in the morning.

The lawyer hadn't been by in a few days, even though before, it felt as though he'd been coming daily. He was probably working, but she wondered if she'd put him off with her curtness last time he'd come.

Cold, uncaring. Echoed accusations stealing from the past to taunt her.

But she couldn't bring herself to be too enthusiastic that he was here either. She didn't really *know* him after all, even if the boys liked him.

Cold...

"Hello the house!" his voice boomed, his round accent filling the corners of the yard with something mellow and friendly. She heard Christopher running to the door to wrench it open.

"*Niit!*" he shouted proudly, and she heard Shawn laugh in delight.

"Much better!" he called back.

She pulled herself away from her paint and went through the house to see Shawn standing in front of the front porch chatting away at Christopher, who was telling him everything from the moose he swore he saw (but no one else had), to the squirrels he was feeding peanuts to, and the birds. Shawn listened attentively, though when Christopher finally stopped for breath, he grinned at Evelyn.

"Afternoon," he said. "Sorry I haven't been by lately. I had work to do with my dad."

"I didn't expect you to come every day," she said, and he looked slightly crestfallen, though it quickly cleared from his dark eyes.

"Of course not," he said, his tone still full of laughter. "But it was rude of me anyway. How are the repairs coming? Get out to Rupert for paint and so on?"

"Yes," she said, mentally chastising herself for being rude. "The Home Hardware there is really good."

He nodded. "Has to be since it serves the whole area," he said. "You haven't been here in the winter storms. There's always some clean-up after. Where's Simon?"

"Probably still in bed," Evelyn sighed. "He's been taking the whole summer holidays and free to heart the last few days."

"Better not sleep too long, or he'll find a flopping salmon in his bed one morning."

"You wouldn't do that, would you?" Christopher asked, wide-eyed at the idea. Shawn didn't answer, but he did wink at the younger boy, making him laugh at the image of his older brother in bed with a fish. Evelyn wrinkled her nose.

"My *nts'Tits* did that to me once," he said, reminiscing. "Grandmother," he answered Christopher's bewildered expression. "I was supposed to go fishing with my brother and my dad, and I didn't want to get out of bed. So, she stuck the fish that we were going to have for breakfast in the blankets with me. That worked to get me up!"

Christopher started laughing again and Shawn chuckled too.

"No fish in the beds please," Evelyn groaned. "I'm not up for fishy smelling laundry."

Shawn grinned. "Fortunately, I'm not his *nts T'its,* so you're all safe. And I don't have a fish with me anyway. I was heading south to do some work for my dad, so I thought I'd drop off the card of my realtor friend Grace, and the last of the bank paperwork since they finally did their end." He looked the house up and down while handing Evelyn a slim folder. "It looks a bit better."

"It's getting there," Evelyn said, flattered. "I was doing some painting inside and the gardener, Kal, has been working on the yard."

"Decided to keep him on then?" Shawn said. "I've never met him. Not sure anyone in the village has. He must live in Terrace or something." He shrugged. "I'll leave you to it then. Tell Simon I said hi. And to watch out for fish." He ruffled Christopher's hair and nodded to Evelyn who had the sudden, wild urge to hug him. She squashed it as quickly as it came, but something must have translated on her face because Shawn gave her a puzzled look.

Fortunately, Christopher chose that moment to loudly point out that he was hungry. She rolled her eyes at Shawn and ushered Christopher inside, closing the door and listening for the jeep to leave.

You're not even officially divorced yet, she scolded herself. *What do you think you're* doing?

She got Christopher settled with some food, checked on Simon who was still sound asleep, and called Zan from the relative safety of her room.

"Hi Evie!" Zan chirped. She sounded slightly distracted, so Evelyn must have caught her in the middle of her work.

"Evie, now?"

She could practically see Zan shrug. "It works. What's up?"

If Zan was asking for information, she was *bored* at work. And Evelyn didn't feel bad about distracting one of the bookkeepers of the business that let her go under such a flimsy pretext.

"Simon is acting more and more like a teenager. And Shawn has been by a lot."

"Simon *is* going to be eleven soon. Those teen years aren't far off now."

Evelyn muttered something foul under her breath.

"And for Shawn, so what? I figured you'd be feeling kinda lonely out there."

"I don't know," Evelyn said, lying flat on her bed, staring at the rough ceiling.

"Bit of a crush?" Zan asked cheerfully. "From what you've told me, he sounds far better than Robert. Lawyer, doesn't drink his weight every day, gorgeous black hair, and that whole man of the land vibe."

Evelyn snorted. "Just because he's Indigenous doesn't make him a 'man of the land'. What does that even *mean*?"

"Who cares?" Zan said. "He sounds dreamy. Bag him."

"I'm still technically *married*," Evelyn hissed. "The divorce won't be finalized for weeks, at least."

"Believe me girl, Robert isn't worth holding on to anything for. He's sunk even lower, if such a thing were possible. Besides, hasn't he agreed to everything, no contest? I mean, you're practically divorced."

"Practically isn't completely. I can't just 'bag' another man."

Zan heaved a massive sigh. "I knew you'd say that. What do you want to do about this, then?"

"I just... needed to hear your voice," Evelyn said. "This place feels empty. And the gardener gives me the creeps."

"Spooky old guy?" Zan guessed. "Probably wears a big hat and has a squinty eye."

"No," Evelyn said in exasperation. "He's not old at all. Just... spooky. I don't see much of him, but the work gets done and he doesn't talk much."

"Also sounds ideal," Zan snickered.

Evelyn shuddered.

"Evelyn, is he... Did he threaten you or something?" Zan asked, suddenly concerned at her friend's silence.

"No," Evelyn said. "He's polite. Just... I don't know what to think of him. The boys said they saw someone in the greenhouse, but there was no one there when I checked, and then he suddenly popped up."

She wasn't about to tell Zan that *she* had seen a weird figure in the yard too.

"Maybe it's just because it's isolated out here, and I'm worried about Simon. He thinks his dad likes his beer more than he likes him."

Zan heaved a massive sigh. "He's not wrong, at least not right now. Robert is... not well. Hasn't been well since his dad died and he got fired. Not that I'm excusing his actions, mind you, because he doesn't deserve to be excused, but there it is."

"He shouldn't feel that way, though."

"And Robert shouldn't be drinking himself to death, you shouldn't have gotten laid off, and I should be showered with money and roses every day," Zan said. "We don't work with the hand we want; we work with the one we have."

Evelyn growled again and Zan sighed. "At least you're close to the ocean and the mountains. It's probably beautiful up there."

"It is," Evelyn said. "But it's lonely. And the house is a bit weird. There's an old butcher room in the basement and the boys won't go there anymore, and they get mad at me when I go downstairs. And the whole place needs work before I decide what to do with it." She closed her eyes. "I think I might have bitten off more than I can chew this time, Zan."

The line went quiet for a moment as Zan mentally digested what she said.

"You can always come home," she finally said. "Put the house up for sale as is, and the let the real estate agent, and the lawyers figure it out. The rest of the money from your uncle, and then from the sale, would help you get set up in a nice apartment down here. Or you could move east to the Okanagan or Kootenays and buy a house outright."

"Ye-es," Evelyn said doubtfully. "I could."

"But you hate giving up on anything," Zan finished. "Otherwise, that divorce would have been finalized six months ago."

Evelyn glared at the ceiling, but it was an old fight, well worn and tired. "Not only that," she said through slightly gritted teeth. "This was my uncle's home, and I don't want it to just go away. I still have fond memories of my uncle and it feels a little... treacherous to just sell it off after only being here a few weeks. I'm probably just imagining things and the boys have always had active imaginations."

"So, you won't leave. What will you do next then?"

Not think too hard about handsome, kind lawyers or spooky gardeners, Evelyn told herself. "I'm going to do what renovations and repairs I can and try to spend more time at the beach. I've never believed in ghosts and things like that before, and I'm not going to start now just because this house is a bit eerie."

"And your lawyer friend?"

"Whatever happens, happens," Evelyn said. "I'm not looking to jump into another relationship when I just got out of one."

"Good point," Zan said and there was a noise like she was drinking water. "Do you need me up there with you?"

Evelyn considered that for a moment. On the one hand, the boys would be thrilled, it would be a buffer between herself and Shawn and the weird house, and Zan always made things more cheerful. On the other hand, she had a strangely protective feeling along with an eerie one – she wasn't ready for anyone else to see the house yet.

"It's a long drive," she said, trying to gently put Zan off the idea. "And the guest room isn't fit for anyone yet. I know you love roughing it, Zan, but this isn't a campground in a national park with a picturesque village nearby. We are in the middle of a forest and mountains and the closest coffee shop is a twenty-minute drive away. And it's an eighteen or twenty hour drive up, which wouldn't give you much time to stay what with work."

Zan huffed out a breath. "You're not wrong about any of that, but you're more important," she said. "You sound like you need someone to back you up."

"It's all right," Evelyn said, trying to inject some positivity into her voice and suspecting she was failing. "I just needed to hear a familiar voice that wasn't the kids."

"Let me know if you do want me to come," Zan urged. "I've never been up that way before and I think I'd like it. Phooey to work."

"Don't let your boss or your clients hear you say that," Evelyn laughed.

"I'm always telling my clients to follow their passions. They can hardly think I wouldn't take my own advice. And I'm thinking of quitting this place anyway. After how they treated you, I don't feel good sticking around."

Evelyn chewed her fingernail. "If I need help, I'll call," she promised, mentally crossing her fingers.

They chatted about inconsequential things for a bit longer and then Zan was pulled off the phone by her boss, leaving Evelyn with a dead sound in her ear and a weight in her stomach. She was already regretting pushing Zan out of the idea to come up, even thought she knew that it hadn't been a good one.

Still, having a friendly face around would have been nice.

***

Simon crept out of his room, drawn by the smell of fresh paint from the room just down the hall, and avoiding the sounds of Shawn and his mom talking. He normally would have wanted to talk to Shawn, but he felt drawn to the room instead. He had always vaguely enjoyed fresh smell, mostly for the possibilities of something new where there was something worn out.

The bedroom was the smallest of all four and there was only a simple bed, which had been pulled out into the middle of the floor so that his mom could paint. The baseboards were neatly stacked in the hall by the door, ready to be replaced as needed or put back. There wasn't much else in the room, but Simon enjoyed the refreshing pale blue paint and the peace with the view of the front yard.

Something drew his attention to one of the corners – a gap in the wall, quite small. His mom would have to fill that in, he figured, but it was fun to think of smugglers putting a gem inside. He wandered over and crouched down, trying to peer inside.

It was pretty dark, but he thought he could make out a strange shape. He reached inside the shallow cavity and pulled out what looked like a small man, all made of bundled sticks and dried plants. He handled it very carefully as it threatened to fall apart in his hands. He peered back in the cavity, but there was nothing more to be seen.

The little stick man gave him a bit of a creepy feeling and he wanted to throw it away, but something stayed his hand. Instead, he took it back to his room. The figure felt oddly sticky and rough, probably from bits of dirt and bark clinging to it. It left his hand feeling rough when he did put it down, and he wiped it on his pants.

The little stick man stared up at the ceiling with tiny painted eyes and he suddenly shuddered and shoved it into his pants pocket to figure out later. It was probably just someone's idea of a joke. He should just throw it away.

Instead, he left it deep in his pocket and went downstairs to see if his mom was starting supper soon. It felt like a small warm spot against his leg, oddly comforting for all its weirdness.

Chapter Eight

Morning dawned sullen with rain and Simon and Christopher arguing slightly over their Switch. Evelyn was upstairs trying *not* to think of her strange dreams. She glanced outside to see Kal studying the dying plants around her back porch, but she looked away just as quickly. She didn't feel at all compelled to go downstairs yet.

A cool whisper of air moved through the kitchen, smelling faintly of mint and flowers. The basement door was ajar and, in the breeze, it opened still more, unnoticed by the occupants of the house. The swirl of air wafted down the stairs, uncertain at first.

Then the stairs creaked, and the smell of mint and roses was replaced by something acrid and foul. Something *thumped* on the stairs, a shadow leaning against the wall, curled tightly.

"I don't want to go down there," came a complaining voice.

"I heard something," an older boy's voice insisted.

"We should tell mom."

Simon snorted. "She didn't believe us last time," he pointed out. "But I heard something on the stairs, didn't you? And what's the door doing open?"

Christopher hugged himself as Simon flung both the back door and basement door wide open, letting the water sunlight inside. It cascaded down the staircase and the smell of sulfur and rot dissipated. Simon blinked as he saw a shadow suddenly vanish, leaving behind the faint smell of roses.

"There was something there," Simon whispered. Christopher chewed the tip of his thumb and Simon had to bat his hand out of his mouth.

"A ghost?" Christopher asked.

Simon scoffed, but there wasn't much feeling behind it.

"We should tell mom."

"Tell her *what?*" Simon demanded. "She won't believe us. She didn't see the man in the greenhouse either."

Christopher looked down the basement stairs and shivered. Simon gently pushed him back and slammed the door closed.

"I think you saved a ghost," Christopher speculated when they were back in the living room. "That shadow looked kind of... squished. And it smelled bad. Then it smelled nice when you opened the door."

Simon shrugged. "I'm still not sure we saw anything," he said uncertainly. "There's nothing down there. Just that butcher room and the big room. And a closet."

"I'm not going in that basement ever again," Christopher said decisively. "I wish we could go back to Coquitlam and live with auntie Zan."

Simon straightened his spine. "Well, we can't," he said firmly. "And maybe we did save that whatever it was, and it might need saving again."

"I don't want to save anyone," Christopher sniffled.

"Don't be a baby," Simon scolded. "I'm not going to make you do it by yourself or anything. Stupid. But this place is cool, other than the weird things. And we haven't seen any whales yet."

Christopher acquiesced the point with a nod. "I still think we should tell mom."

"Go ahead," Simon challenged. "See how far you get."

Christopher glared at him, and Simon shrugged.

***

Zan Corshire was not a woman who let things go easily.

She'd be the first to tell anyone she wouldn't let go of something without a fight: not her friends, not ideas that mattered to her, and sometimes a grudge slid in there too, just to make things interesting. She tried not to let those stick around, though the one against Evelyn's ex had some amazing staying power.

She wasn't about to let her friend stay in the wilds of the northwest coast without anyone she knew for much longer. And she missed the boys.

Of course, she couldn't just *leave*. She had her clients to wrap up, her two-week letter of resignation to turn in (that felt satisfying, and then she cashed in her vacation and dared them to do something about it), and then she had to clean the truck, gas it up, and pack to go. Not knowing where she was going wasn't going to stop her when she had a perfectly good Google maps app and a highway lined with mountains and wild rivers beckoning her north. Indeed, once she finished up the last bit of paperwork she didn't entrust to anyone, she bid adieu to the store she'd worked in for several years, and put Coquitlam behind her.

Hitting massive delays between Hope and 100 Mile House slowed her down and she was forced to find a hotel in Quesnel, trundling into the small town late at night and trying not to curse her luck. She would have preferred to stay in Prince George where she would have her choice of restaurants, but the hotel was clean and the night was quiet.

Won't Evelyn be surprised!

***

As Zan was sorting through her belongings and daydreaming of the coast, Evelyn was mostly feeling exasperated and bewildered.

"I don't understand," she said. She had been trying to get the boys to go bed for over an hour. Christopher was known for getting stubborn about it sometimes, but Simon was usually more or less resigned to his fate. She suspected him of reading under the covers, but it was a fair compromise for a few hours of peace, so long as he got up for school. This time, though, both boys were holding a united front: they weren't going to bed.

At first, they tried ignoring her. Then they dragged on having their showers and brushing their teeth. Then they kept asking for more time to finish reading or playing with toys. She tried threats, cajoling, and outright begging: nothing worked until she flat out *asked* and then got mumbled answers.

"There are weird noises in the attic," Christopher finally complained and Simon, much to her surprise, nodded in agreement.

"There's nothing *in* the attic to *make* a weird noise," Evelyn said. She'd gone up there a few days after they arrived. There was nothing there but boxes under old sheets and a dirty mirror and a couple of windows.

"I heard thumping," Simon said, and Christopher nodded.

"Maybe something fell over," Evelyn said. "Some of those boxes weren't very steady."

"That would make only one thump," Simon pointed out. "This was a few of them. Like footsteps."

Evelyn crossed her arms. "Have you boys been reading ghost stories to each other again?"

They both shook their heads, eyes wide. Simon's hair looked even more tousled than usual. He'd been running his hands through it, which he only did when he was worried.

"If I *show* you that there's nothing there, will you please go to bed?"

"There's definitely something there," Simon said. "You shouldn't go up there."

"Well, we can't just stay down here all night," Evelyn pointed out. She went to the kitchen, grabbed the large flashlight since the attic light was erratic at best, and made her way to the pull cord for the ladder.

She was about as happy about doing this as her boys were. She'd only been in the attic once, just to reassure herself that there were no mice, rats or other vermin living there. Once she had ascertained that the only living things in the house were humans, she decided she had no more reason to go up there and avoided it, planning to leave it alone for the rest of the summer.

But the boys weren't going to sleep until she proved there was nothing to be scared of, so she yanked on the cord to drop the door, opened up the stepladder and flicked the flashlight on. The boys crowded around her, and she gave them a reassuring smile before turning to her task, grateful that it was only a few steps to get up.

The darkness crawled out from the open attic door, reaching down with alien fingers to creep across her spine. Despite the fear that suddenly caused her heart to thud loudly in her ears, she climbed partway up the ladder and tried to stare through the gloom.

"There's nothing up there but dust," she said, trying to avoid continuing up. "I don't hear anything."

Christopher took his thumb out of his mouth. "Mama," he said uncertainly. "I don't like it."

Even Simon gave the open space above Evelyn a deeply suspicious look and stood in front of his brother. "I heard noises up there too," he said firmly. "Christopher wasn't just making things up."

Evelyn sighed and finished climbing the ladder, clambering into the attic properly. *Probably mice,* she told herself.

"It's never mice!" Zan's voice echoed in her memory from the last horror movie they watched. She shook it off.

The attic was covered in a thick layer of dust and a spider skittered away from the beam of light she cast about as she moved a few feet from the entrance. There was nothing more eerie than some boxes, a few covered pieces of furniture, and the window that could only let in splinters of early moonlight.

"There's nothing up here," she said firmly and started back for the ladder. The dust made her want to sneeze and there was the smell of old mould and a dry, itchy feeling on her skin.

The feeling of something watching her suddenly crashed over her. She turned again and saw pinpoints of reflected light staring at her.

Rats! She thought, but when she shone the flashlight in that direction, expecting to see a fleeing, furry body, she saw something twisted and broken instead, the ruins of what could have been a person, staring at her with mad eyes. It hurled itself at her and she screamed and fell back onto the ladder, gathering enough of her wits to pull the attic door closed behind her as she tumbled down the ladder.

But she heard, and felt, something bashing at the door, trying to come through. Christopher burst into tears and Simon grabbed her arm, trying to pull her away.

The attic door seemed to bulge under the thing's fury, and then it abruptly went still and silent. Evelyn heard a final sound like a gasp of air, then silence from above them.

The attic door looked normal. If it hadn't been for the scrapes Evelyn had on her hands from nearly falling down the ladder, she might have thought she'd somehow imagined the whole thing.

They camped out in the living room that night, but there wasn't a single sound to be heard and only moonlight broke the gloom.

A final strange thought chased Evelyn into an uneasy sleep.

Did I smell... sage?

Chapter Nine

Morning had never been greeted with as much relief as it was when the family woke up. Evelyn was relieved to see that the boys had managed to drop off to sleep despite everything, and when they woke up, Simon was only a bit distant, and Christopher kept nearly tripping over things.

"I know that the prospect of going back to Coquitlam may not be appealing when we've only been here for a few weeks," Evelyn said over breakfast. "But I don't think there's much for us. I can hire someone to fix up the rest of the place and put it on the market. We don't need to stay here all summer."

Christopher nodded fiercely, but Simon looked up at Evelyn.

"No," he said.

Evelyn blinked at him. "What?"

"No. I don't want to leave. I don't think we *should* leave, and I won't leave."

"You can't stay here by yourself," Evelyn said lightly.

"Then I guess you're staying here too." And with that, Simon got up and went upstairs before Evelyn could get her thoughts together to argue the point.

Christopher looked nervous. "Simon doesn't want to go back home," he said. "Even with the scary thing in the attic. He likes the forest."

"It's also the forest I'm worried about," Evelyn said, still staring in the direction her eldest had gone.

She could hardly *drag* him to the car and tie him down. At eleven years old, he was only a couple of inches shorter than her and while he wasn't an overly muscular child, he was lanky and would fight back if he really felt pressed into it. She doubted she could physically force him to go anywhere he truly didn't want to go.

Besides, despite the scare of the night before, she could feel the same reluctance dragging at her. It was a feeling of not quite fear, but anxiety about going much farther than Prince Rupert, and even then, the idea of being gone long made her worry. She closed her eyes for a moment.

There's no reason to feel that way. This wasn't meant to be your house and you never intended to keep it. Coquitlam is your home. This is not your home.

It didn't help and the thought of someone *else* living here filled her with a combination of fear and anger. She took another deep breath and opened her eyes to see Christopher looked worriedly at her.

"It'll be all right," she reassured him. "Simon will come around, you'll see. And we never meant to stay here longer than the summer. He's just acting out. There's been a lot of changes lately." *If I have to get Shawn to drag him to the van, I will.*

Christopher didn't look convinced, but since all he could really say was 'What if he isn't just acting out' and Evelyn had no answer for that, they couldn't say much more to each other on the topic. Evelyn listened for her eldest son, but he must have put himself back to bed. And she knew he didn't go outside since both the doors of the house loudly creaked.

"Let me know if you see or hear anything else," she said to Christopher who was reluctantly sliding off his chair. "Whatever is going on here, we'll get to the bottom of it."

"What was that thing in the attic?" Christopher asked. "Will it... hurt us?"

She could feel her mental foundation cracking slightly out from under her and she put a tight leash on the memory of the *thing* crawling towards her.

"Whatever is going here," she said slowly. "We must stay together. I will always protect both of you. And we'll get out of here as soon as we can, all right?"

Christopher gave her a hug and left to play with his toys outside. He was playing in the backyard where the greenhouse, which still felt like there was something unseen lurking nearby, had an oddly reassuring feel to it rather than creepy.

Evelyn took another deep breath and then went upstairs to check on her eldest son.

The bedroom door was resolutely closed, and she took a moment to stare at it. The wood was scored as though many people had banged on it, or a dog had scratched it, leaving scars in the wood. It was one more thing to replace, though at the moment, it suited its surroundings. The unhappiness from Simon seemed to seep under the door, filling his mother with dread. She knocked, waited a moment, and then slowly opened the door.

Simon didn't bring anything to decorate his room with, but his mark was there. There were a couple of large jars filled with sticks, dirt, and insects. There was a shelf that was partly full of odd branches and drying mushrooms that filled the air with a pungent odour that covered the normal smell of adolescent. His floor had a light coating of dirty laundry while the object of her concern lay on his back on the bed, covers kicked aside, staring at the ceiling.

"Simon?" she said uncertainly.

He rolled over and presented his back to her.

Well, at least I know he's still alive, she thought, and while normally that line of thinking would be entirely hyperbolic, this time she mostly just felt grateful.

"Simon, I know you're enjoying your time here, but..." Her voice trailed and she sighed. "Well, I know this place has captured your imagination."

"We can't go," he said, sounding muffled. "We *can't.*"

She wasn't sure what to say. The bone-deep conviction in his voice told her that nothing she did, short of tying him up and throwing him in the SUV, would make him leave. She didn't know if he would then just spend the rest of his teens yearning for the old house and the woods until he could move back under his own power.

The thought terrified her, and she dragged herself back to cool logic. Of course, he would bounce back. This was normal push-back, normal grieving. She *knew* this. Zan had *warned* her he would act out when she first started the process of divorcing Robert. She'd also told Evelyn that fighting with Simon would just make everything worse.

"We're not going right now," she said. "I don't even know where we will live. We can't keep staying with Zan after all. I have to figure that out first."

He rolled over to look at her. "That'll take her a while, won't it?"

Not if I have anything to say about it, she thought. "At least longer than this week," she compromised.

He suddenly grinned and it was like the sun came out. "Good," he said, bouncing out of bed. "I'm hungry."

Evelyn laughed a little and he led the way back to the kitchen to finish his breakfast.

***

Evelyn had only seen Kal a few times since she'd decided to keep him on, and it was always in the morning when he was most active. Today, though, he seemed strangely exhausted and was leaning against the greenhouse when she came out.

Even his dark hair looked lank, and his strange eyes were sunken.

"Are you okay?" she asked.

He jumped a little, which surprised her; she didn't think of the man as someone who could be easily startled and she'd hardly been sneaking.

"I'm sorry," he said, rubbing his eyes. "Late night."

She raised an eyebrow at him and noticed that his knuckles were bruised and scratched up. He turned them away from her curious gaze as best he could, but it was too late.

"I didn't think there was anywhere around here to get into a fight," she said lightly. *Or that you were the type*.

"You'd be surprised," he said, picking up his rake. "Friday nights, there's not always much else to do but drink and get into fights."

"Do you need the day off?"

He yawned and stretched. The morning sunlight cast the shadows around him in such a way that for a moment *her* tired imagination filled in strange shapes that reached up towards the sky to greet the blue.

"No," he said, bringing her attention back to reality with a bump. "*I* wasn't the one drinking. It wasn't a difficult fight to win either – caught the bastard unaware." He smiled an almost secretive smile that was more to himself than her and she gave him a bewildered look. He started to walk away with the rake over his shoulder and then stopped and looked back at her.

"You are my employer and I know very little about you," he said. "We should fix that. I'd like to know more about you and where you come from."

She took a step back. "Why?"

"Isn't that a thing that is done?" he asked. "Telling each other about ourselves?"

"Are we the kind of people who do that?" she asked, flustered.

He shrugged. "Are we the kind of people who *don't?*" he returned. "If you're going to be here for a while and paying my way, I think I should know something about you. There have been odd people here before."

"You mean my uncle," she said flatly.

His hazel eyes flickered gold for a moment. "Yes," he said. "Your uncle. Are you uncomfortable telling me about yourself?"

"I don't usually tell people I don't know all about myself."

He smirked at her. "Then how do you get to know anyone? We don't have to *go* anywhere. I'll meet you here after I'm done." With that, he walked away again, and she was left spluttering in his wake.

He had a point about getting to know more about the person she was paying, but it felt as thought she'd been tricked into something.

Evelyn fully intended to use painting and renovations as an excuse to not go outside for the rest of the day, but she realized at around noon that she had left some of her gear on the back porch. She didn't check the time, but when she went outside to get her brushes, Kal was sitting on the steps, his long legs trailing down.

"I came to get my brushes," she said immediately.

"They're over there," he said in amusement as she sidled behind him and gathered them up in her arms. She turned back and tried to open the door back into the house, but it was stuck.

"It's not funny," she hissed as the paintbrushes clattered around her feet. She yanked ineffectually at the stuck door.

"I didn't say it was," he said mildly. "I can take those around to the front door for you."

She *wanted* to refuse him, but realized she would be playing out the same scene around the front. Stiffly, she nodded and let him gather up the thick brushes and led him around the house.

"You don't have to tell me everything about yourself," he said. "Tell me *one* thing."

"One thing?"

"Just one. Something about yourself that you are proud of. What would you tell an employee that is important?"

"You're nosy."

"That is something about me, yes," he said, his voice turning amused again. "Some have accused me of... nosiness."

She looked behind her and he was smiling his secret smile again, eyes glittering.

"They're right," she snapped, feeling wrong-footed.

"And you?"

Evelyn snarled under her breath. "I don't know what to tell you. Or why I should."

"Your boys?" he suggested. "Or about Coquitlam?"

"Leave my boys out of this," she snapped and then felt somewhat stupid.

"*I* mean your boys no harm," he said and that stopped her short.

"Why would you say that?" she asked as he reached her side.

"Reassurance."

"The way you said it..."

He gazed steadily at her, and she growled under her breath. "I'm not telling you anything," she said. "I'm probably going to sell this place soon and we will *never* see each other again. Coming out here was a mistake."

He studied her. "So, why not leave and sell the place as is? Surely someone will buy it for the land, if nothing else."

Something crawled up her spine at the thought. "I..." she muttered. "I don't want that."

He looked up at the house. "I imagine you don't."

They reached the front door and she opened it a crack to make sure it wouldn't jam up as well. Then she took her brushes back. "Thanks," she said, feeling ashamed of her behaviour. He stood a respectful few feet away from her.

"You're welcome," he said. "Be careful, Evelyn."

She firmly shut the door on him, but it was several moments before she heard him going back down the stairs. The adrenaline fled her body and she leaned against the wall trying to catch her breath. The boys were still in the living room playing video games. She listened to them argue for a moment, just to reassure herself that everything was normal. Then she went back to the room she was painting, but found she no longer had the heart for it.

***

For a few days, Shawn was distracted from the house by other things. His father had work for him: interviews to conduct, research on the impact sites to prove that the new fishery could not be built where the company wanted it to go, and paperwork to finish. He was mostly certain that his father and the band had a good case to tell the commercial fishery to take a hike, but there was always a nasty lingering concern that they'd pull something unexpected that would ruin their arguments, so he spent a few days plugging holes.

This meant spending a lot of time in Port Edward as the rain dripped from gray skies. He didn't normally mind, but the village seemed particularly sullen of late. He wasn't even greeted with the usual enthusiasm from the locals. Even his own cousins spoke to him civilly enough when he saw them, but with none of the usual ribbing about his status as a single man and the mocking demands that he come out to Terrace to see a hockey game and drink beer.

Shawn didn't quite feel welcome in the village where he'd been raised, and he wasn't sure why.

He was at the post office sipping what might have been his third or fifth coffee of the day and watching the afternoon clouds *finally* part for the sun when a small truck rumbled into the village. He didn't recognize it, though it was dirty enough to be local. Where most people here though drove white, black, or red trucks, this one was an almost eye-searing shade of bright blue under the layer of dirt. The truck rolled to a stop and out barrelled a woman that Port Edward had never before seen the likes of.

About four inches shorter than Shawn, who was not a tall man himself, with a crown of red-gold hair, she sized him up with brown eyes and put her hands on her hips. He stared back at her, and she sauntered towards him.

Even the crows on the powerlines above him fell silent at her approach as though stunned by the mane of autumn hair and the crackling energy she radiated.

"*Well*," she said, holding out a hand for him to shake. "I'm glad to finally see someone! I was worried I was lost, but I've also just about run out of road."

He laughed and she grinned at him. "I'm Zan."

"Shawn," he returned, shaking her hand. "Where are you *trying* to go?"

She checked her phone. "South of Port Edward somewhere," she said. "Is *this* Port Edward?"

Shawn felt a chill go down his spine. "You're here to see Evelyn, right?" he asked. "She's the only one who lives south of here. You're going in the right direction."

"Oh good," she said warmly and then did a double take and studied him. "What's wrong?"

He shook himself and smiled. "Nothing. If you follow the main road south and then keep going, you'll find the driveway to the house about four kilometres from here. It's pretty wide, so you shouldn't miss it. Then drive up a couple kilometres and you'll see the house."

"Thanks," Zan said, but she still looked uneasily at Shawn who tried to keep the smile plastered on his face. She narrowed her eyes. "*Something* is wrong."

He huffed out a sigh. "It's nothing," he insisted. "I assume you are Evelyn's friend."

"Of course," she said. "Why *else* would I have driven almost two thousand clicks to get here? Evelyn is my best friend."

Shawn chewed his lip and Zan continued to study him. Then she snapped her fingers.

"Shawn *Myers*. You're the lawyer she's working with about the house."

Sideswiped by her recognition of him, he blinked. "I guess she's been talking about me?"

"Yeah," Zan said. "She said you've been visiting her a lot."

He crossed his arms over his chest. "Just making sure she's alright," he said defensively. "She's pretty remote now compared to what she'd be used to down south. And the house isn't in the best shape."

"Uh huh," she said. He glared at her, and she grinned and hopped back into her truck. "Thanks!"

"You're welcome," he said and shook his head as she drove away, heading south.

"*She had skoden eyes!*" One of his cousin's voices came into his head and he chuckled. Zan certainly did seem like the type who would barrel through anyone and anything in her way.

That might be exactly what Evelyn needed to feel safe in that house. And that meant Shawn lost another excuse to be up there.

The crows on the telephone wires overhead cawed derisively and he sighed.

"You're probably right," he told them.

Zan kept glancing in her rear-view mirror as the man who had directed her receded into the distance. He was still leaning on his jeep, staring up at several crows. She whistled a little under her breath. "Way to go Evie," she muttered, though it seemed her best friend wasn't about to hop on that wagon any time soon.

He hadn't precisely been *her* type, though for that head of thick black hair, bright smile, and intelligent dark eyes, she might be convinced otherwise. She did appreciate him looking out for Evelyn and the boys.

Shawn and Port Edward quickly faded from view as she was plunged back into a corridor of trees and hills, with the ocean flickering in and out of sight. It was very peaceful and Zan rolled down her window to enjoy the cool breeze and the smell of green trees and sea salt. *If I had inherited a house out here, I'm not sure I'd ever want to leave. But I guess Evelyn has always been more of a city girl.* Still, she hoped that even a city slicker like Evelyn had been won over a little by her surroundings. She sounded nervous on the phone, but Zan chalked that up to being somewhere new while still in the middle of a divorce.

At about the point Shawn had said it would be, the driveway showed itself on the left-hand side, a gash in the trees. She carefully turned onto it, paying close attention to the ruts and potholes, and began her slow and steady ascent. The tree branches whacked against her windows, and she had to slow down or risk bottoming out. She wondered how Evelyn's vehicle was faring on this road as even her truck was bouncing, especially when she let her attention wander.

She hit a mostly clear stretch of road and let her attention do just that for a moment. It wandered over to the trees on her left. She told herself it was to watch for moose or deer, but the brush was so thick she doubted she'd be able to see an animal even if it was two feet away. She did see *something*, though, and she slammed on the brakes and screeched to a halt, then slowly backed the truck up to look again.

It was a strange stick figure hanging from the branch of a tree, slowly turning in the light breeze. As she squinted at it, she realized with a shudder that it wasn't made from twigs like the ones she and her girlfriends used to make when they were kids during the Blair Witch Project mania. This one was made from what looked to be bones, red thread tying them together, giving them shape. It was just deep enough in the trees that she'd have to get out and make her way over to get a proper look.

Normally, Zan would have done just that, but something about the small white and gray figure signing in the breeze gave her the absolute creeps. She rolled up her windows, locked her doors, and continued up the road instead.

Must be a prank or something, she told herself. *Or have some meaning to a single person. It's nothing to do with Evelyn.*

She had the crawling feeling that if she looked behind her, there would be more of the small, sinister figures swinging in the trees, so she kept her gaze resolutely forward until the house came into view.

The house didn't exactly make her feel better.

Had the two-storey building been in *town*, she might have called it ramshackle, but thought nothing further of it. If she'd been with a few of her friends, she might have called it rustic.

In the middle of the forest with the sun setting, it looked foreboding. The attic window glared vacantly down at her, the door looked too big, and even Evelyn's van was dwarfed by the building's presence. The late sunlight reflecting from the windows looked reddish orange like eyes brooding at her.

Overactive imagination, she scolded herself. It was just a bit of a battered house with the potential for something interesting once it was repaired. Evelyn had probably just gotten herself a small fortune, certainly enough to return to the lower mainland or live somewhere else once this place was fixed up and sold. Or maybe it could be used as a lodge for hunting or skiing.

Realizing her mind was going in circles when she should be going to the house to surprise her best friend, she took a hard swallow of the last of her soda, unlocked her truck door and hopped out. The cool breeze slapped her face and she shivered. There was *nothing* weird here. It was just a run-down house in beautiful surroundings.

In any event, Evelyn did not need, or want, her hysterical imagination. She strode up to the door, but before she could knock, it was flung open by an excited four-year-old.

"Auntie Zan, auntie Zan!" Christopher babbled and she laughed and picked him up. He flung his arms around her neck and nearly crushed her windpipe before squirming to be put down again. "You came!"

"I had to see the place that has everyone so enraptured," Zan said. "Where's your mom?"

"Right here," Evelyn said, her eyes wide with surprise at seeing Zan on her front porch. "I didn't know you were coming!"

"I thought I'd surprise you," Zan said, embracing her friend. She noted with a mental frown that Evelyn had lost weight. Her shoulders seemed too boney and there was a wan look to her face that she was trying to hide. There was no sign of Simon.

"I don't even have the guest room ready," Evelyn stuttered.

Zan shrugged. "I can sleep on a couch. I'm not here to be a guest; I'm here to help."

Evelyn chewed her lip, but stood aside to let Zan in.

Zan whistled as she looked around the house. "This is a nice place," she said, sitting down at the kitchen table. "Little run down, but lots of potential."

"That's what I thought," Evelyn said, relaxing a little as Zan looked around the room and stretched, cat-like, in the last of the sunshine. "There's definitely something here to work with and I could use the money to get my own place down south."

Or stay here forever.

The thought was intrusive, but as she looked around, the urge to sell was growing fainter and fainter. Zan didn't seem to notice anything. She leaned back in her chair, let Christopher climb on her lap, and smiled. "I met Shawn."

Evelyn forced herself back into the conversation before she could say something incriminating. "Oh?"

"He pointed the way here," Zan said. "Seemed nice. Port Edward has almost nothing to it, does it? I think I blinked and missed most of it. But the harbour was lovely and I think I saw some nice walking paths."

"There's a pretty good bakery too," Evelyn said, standing up and starting supper. She wasn't feeling very hungry, but Zan was probably starving, and the boys always wanted to eat. One of the frozen lasagnas was easy. "You'll probably like Prince Rupert better and it's not far."

"We'll have to go soon," Zan said decisively and then, as though psychically attuned to her 'nephews', she swivelled around to wave Simon into the room. He had been peering around the doorway and he frowned, but he also wasn't about to let his brother get all the attention, so he sidled into the kitchen.

"How are you, Simon?" Zan asked warmly, bumping Christopher gently off her lap so she could stand up.

He shrugged and looked at his feet.

"I thought I'd come for a visit," she said. Simon's reticence unnerved her. Normally, he would have started taking her ear off about the stuff he found in the forest, but this time he was completely closed in. He did sit at the table, but he didn't seem interested in talking.

In fact, Zan was starting to get the feeling she wasn't welcome. Even the house made her feel as though it was studying her like a bug.

She firmly put it out of her head. Bad energy or not, she was here to support Evelyn and the boys, not to prove herself to a damn house.

Evelyn was trying to act normally, but the conversation regularly tapered to silence and Simon was sullen throughout. Christopher chattered about the new words he learned from Shawn, about the bear he thought he saw and the squirrels he was feeding. But even he couldn't keep the conversation going alone and by the time supper ended, any chance at talk ended too.

When they were outside watching the sun set, Evelyn seemed to come back to herself. She nursed her tea and stared at the greenhouse.

"I'm glad you came," she said. "But I don't know if it was a good idea."

"Why?"

"There's... I don't even know how to tell you," she said, sagging in on herself. "This house is..." She closed her eyes. "Haunted? Something is *wrong*. And there's a... well, the boys say anyway, there's something in the greenhouse. And something in the *attic*." She shook her head. "I don't even know what I'm saying. Maybe there's something biological going on, like gas or fungus or something."

Zan snickered. "*Fungus?*"

Evelyn managed a smile, but it was a weak one. "You'll see. Though I hope you won't."

Zan leaned over the porch railing, staring out at the trees. "Why don't you just leave?"

"I don't know. Simon refuses. That doesn't help. And... This was my uncle's house. I should at least clean it up and find a good buyer for it. And it's not all bad. The scenery is beautiful, and the people are friendly enough so far."

"Especially Shawn," Zan said, chuckling.

Evelyn waved a hand. "I don't want to leave so soon. And I don't want to go back to Coquitlam yet. Too many bad memories."

Zan nodded. "I get it. Simon is going through some things, you know. I'm sure he'll come around. He's probably just enjoying all the peace away from Rob's drinking. And he's always enjoyed being out in the wilderness."

Evelyn didn't know how to voice everything going through her mind, and what she worried was going through Simon's mind, so she nodded. Zan gave her a doubtful look.

"If there's something going on here, I'll help you figure it out," she said. She held out her fist for Evelyn to bump, just as they had ever since they were teenagers.

She was unsurprised, but sad, when Evelyn didn't bump her fist, and the conversation died.

Chapter Ten

Shawn's father had moved to Prince Rupert when he opened his practice, and when Shawn moved back to British Columbia, he tried to convince his son to do the same. However, Shawn refused to leave Port Edward. Even though many of his cousins and other family treated him terribly, he still felt beholden to keep an eye on them, so he stayed in the village, mostly ignored, but vigilant.

Therefore, Shawn was very startled when he returned home from a fishing trip to see his dad sitting at his scuffed kitchen table looking worried. He had a key of course, but he had never intruded on his son's privacy. It had to be serious.

"Is everything all right?" Shawn asked immediately, dropping the empty cooler on the floor with a rattle.

"Have you seen Lori in the last few days?"

Shawn shook his head. "I haven't seen her since she got dumped here a week or so ago."

"*No* one has seen her for a few days," Aaron said. "Not her usual boyfriends, not Liz, not any of her friends. She said she was going back to her trailer?"

"That's what she told me," Shawn said, feeling sick. He should have *checked* on her, but he'd been busy with the practice and the strange house in the mountains, and anyway, she never appreciated him hanging around her place. She nearly threw a shoe at him once. "Have the cops been called?"

Aaron waved a hand and snorted.

"Someone must have seen her lately," Shawn pressed. "She couldn't have just vanished."

"I just assumed she was out partying again or even went to Terrace, but her usual rides said they haven't heard from her. And take a look at this." Aaron slid his phone over to Shawn who looked down to see Lori's Facebook page.

The last post was dated for the night before.

"He said I would forget."

This was followed by a stream of comments ranging from praising her turn of phrase to wondering what was going on, often in more colourful language. Prior to that, there had been nothing since the party she had been at before stumbling into Shawn's house, except for one post that succinctly said, "Fuck you."

"She broke up with Trevor," Shawn said. "Dumped him, or so she claimed. Maybe it was actually worse than that."

Aaron's face darkened. "Trevor wasn't just her latest boyfriend. I'm pretty sure he was her dealer."

Shawn gulped. "Pot is legal now," he offered. "Been for a while."

Aaron shook his head at his son. "She's gone beyond pot." He rubbed his arm meaningfully and Shawn choked on his drink. "You see why I'm worried? And who said she would forget and what is she forgetting?"

Shawn sighed. "She was probably stoned out of her mind," he pointed out. "Wouldn't be the first time. Or... worse, I guess. Wherever she is, she has internet. She's probably sleeping somewhere."

Aaron shook his head. "I don't like it," he said. "This isn't like Lori."

That much was true. Prior to the party post, she posted daily – usually stupid memes and quizzes, heavily splattered with jokes, swearing, and selfies. Then the party, the brief expletive and nothing until the night before.

"How was she acting when you saw her?" Aaron pressed.

"She was drunk," Shawn said. "So, about normal. And the next morning, she was hung over. I fed her and went to work and when I came home, she was gone. I just assumed she went home."

Aaron sighed.

"I'm sure she's fine, dad," Shawn said. "She was able to post last night, so it's not like she's up in the mountains or being held hostage or something."

They both glanced reflexively east, towards Highway 16 headed to Prince George, the notorious Highway of Tears.

"She wouldn't have hitchhiked anywhere," Shawn said immediately. "She always asks for rides from her friends, you know that. I'm sure she's just sleeping off a binge, hence the weird post. Maybe one of her other dealers told her that something they wanted to sell her would make her forget whatever's bothering her. She's probably still mooning over Trevor, especially if he was supplying her with her latest addiction."

"Maybe," Aaron said, but he still didn't look satisfied, and Shawn couldn't blame him.

"I should get back home," he said reluctantly. "Keep an eye out, okay?"

"I will, dad," Shawn promised. "I'll cruise around and see if I can find her. She probably won't thank us for it though."

"I'll feel better knowing she's safe. Or..." It was unsaid, but they both knew what Aaron was thinking: *'At least knowing where her body is, if not her.'*

The house felt sombre after his dad left and Shawn felt sick to his stomach. He had to firmly shake himself. *She posted last night. She was alive last night, she's alive now.*

And he knew his cousin pretty well, he figured; at least enough to maybe find hiding spots that no one else knew about. He wasn't going to be able to eat supper now, so he grabbed his keys and headed back into the late afternoon haze.

His dad and her friends who could have been roused would have combed Port Edward, but he knew of a few spots outside the village where she sometimes went, especially when she wanted to be alone. The beach held a few tiny coves and there was a ruined cabin she was vaguely fixing up. However, all her hiding spots were empty, waves and wind whistling through them as though mourning his cousin. He stood just outside the cabin and tapped his keys against his thigh, trying to think where else she could have gone on foot.

Even Lori wouldn't have gone stumbling into the woods, would she? It seemed unlikely. Even as a child, she'd been more drawn to the ocean than the trees. He gave the waves a suspicious look, but there was no sign of a body washed up on shore. Then, as though being dragged against his will, he looked back at the woods.

"Fuck," he said, and went to get his jeep.

He drove up and down the south road, and even walked into the trees a little, calling her name, but as darkness rolled over the mountains, he had to give up the search. There was no sign of her anywhere.

I'll go to Evelyn's in the morning and see if she's seen anyone, he decided, swinging back into his vehicle, and giving the trees around him a dark look. The branches rattled, seemingly in response.

***

There was a woman standing at the edge of the trees in the deepening shadows.

Simon was supposed to be in bed, and for a moment, he thought he had fallen asleep and was dreaming. He'd been tired all day and even though Zan would normally have cheered him up, her presence hadn't permeated the gray gloom that had drawn a curtain over his mind. He found that he just didn't care, so he put himself to bed rather than fight with his mother over it.

The cool wood threatening slivers under his hands told him he was awake and there actually was a bedraggled looking woman standing at the treeline, staring at the house.

It wasn't the same woman he'd seen out in the forest. She was solid, unlike the girl in the woods, though her hair was also black. She looked older, though still younger than his mom. She was very skinny under her baggy clothes. She looked a bit like Shawn, if Shawn didn't care of himself. He pressed his nose against the window, but she wasn't looking at him. She rubbed one arm vaguely.

He was sure she was in some kind of trouble.

Simon's window did open, but it opened on a rather rickety part of the roof and from there, it was a good twelve-foot drop to the ground. He had been poking around, though, and had found an old trellis that creaked and rocked alarmingly, but held his weight as long as he was careful. He was slightly less cautious now and ended up dropping the last few feet as the trellis gave way beneath him. He winced and tears sprang into his eyes as he landed badly on his knees, but nothing seemed to be damaged, so he made his way across the yard, keeping an eye out for his mother, Zan, or worse, Christopher.

The woman finally noticed him, but her dark eyes were weirdly vacant, much like his dad's were when he his drinking hit the right tipping point at midnight.

"Do you need help?" he asked. Her feet were bare and filthy from the forest floor and while her hoodie looked thick, her leggings were not. "I can get my mom to call someone."

"He told me to come here," she said vaguely, and he frowned.

"You shouldn't be here without shoes," he said firmly, trying to channel his mother.

That got a bit of a response from her. She stared down at her feet as though surprised to see them.

"I came here to pay," she said, looking back up. "Do you take me?"

"Noooo," Simon said, backing up a pace. "Definitely not. I'm going to get mom." He moved back, but she followed him, so they remained the same distance apart. Her eyes were vacant again, her movements dreamy.

There was a chill at his back, and he turned his head to see that the house was a lot closer than he thought it was. Part of him wanted to run for the back door, but he also didn't want to turn his back on the strange woman who had stopped again and was staring up at the attic window.

"Mom!" he tried to shout, but his throat felt choked, and it only came out as a whisper. "Mom!" She had to hear. She *always* heard him, even when he was under the blankets, sobbing in fear from nightmares.

The attic window clattered, but otherwise there was no sign of life from the house. He backed up a few more steps, but the woman's attention was entirely on the attic window. She raised her arms as though trying to reach up to climb the walls. The attic window banged and he yelled, trying to scare off either the woman, or the thing making noise in his house; he wasn't sure which. But since it had mostly come out as a squeak, he knew it wouldn't work.

His mother was nowhere to be seen.

The attic window crashed open, and *something* flooded out – dark, cold, and hungry. It looked mostly like a shadow, but his mind happily filled in the details: sharp teeth, red eyes, grasping hands, and limbs where limbs ought not to be. It rode the shadows cast by the house over his head and down to the woman, covering her like a sheet.

He was frozen in place and dimly humiliated to feel a warmth trickling down his leg. No one was coming to pat his back, tuck him in or turn on the lights and reassure him that it was all in his head.

For a moment, the stranger simply stood, her features still empty, while the shadow spilled around her in a tight chain, and then it fled and she fell to her knees, suddenly looking exhausted.

Simon shook himself. *What am I doing outside?* And then, horrified, *I wet myself?!*

There was a stranger collapsed in the yard and he went inside to wake up his mother and get help. But he changed his pyjamas first, burying them in his laundry basket, and by the time he managed to get Evelyn awake and outside, the stranger had disappeared.

"Did you have a bad dream?" Evelyn asked blearily, staring around the dark yard.

Something with teeth and too many arms. A woman.

"Maybe," Simon said. "I was sure, though..." A feeling of horror and betrayal still lurked in his chest. He didn't want to look at his mother.

"Come inside," Evelyn gently urged, now feeling more worried about her oldest son. "It's cold out here."

Both relieved and reluctant, Simon followed her back inside.

Behind the greenhouse, the woman lay sprawled half in the ground, a ring glittering in the waning moonlight. The greenhouse door creaked open and golden eyes peered out, then narrowed. There was a puff of displaced air and the body slowly finished sinking into the earth.

"*Requiescat in pace.*"

Chapter Eleven

It was raining the next morning, which came as no surprise to Shawn, but as he hit the road south to the old house, the sky grew darker and soon he was accompanied by rumbles of thunder. He turned up the speed of the wipers and looked uneasily around. This would be a bad place for lightning to take a tree down. The wind began to shudder around him, setting the fir and spruce trees swaying.

He turned onto the driveway and slowed down. The rain was coming steadily now, a true soaking in the tradition of the northwest coast. He kept a close eye on his surroundings. It was unlikely any animals would come darting out of the brush in this rain, but one never knew.

Keeping an eye out for moose made him notice something else: a strange figure made from what looked to be light coloured sticks and dark thread, hanging in a tree. He frowned and hit the brakes. No one was coming up behind him anyway, and he wasn't going far.

The strange figure was dangling a couple of inches above his head; he had to stand on his tip toes to brush it with his fingers. The thing felt slimy, and he recoiled.

"It's just from the rain," he muttered, though this close, he could see that the figure wasn't made with sticks, but with small animal bones, perhaps bird or mouse.

He had a flashback to being a teenager and watching The Blair Witch Project with all of its stick figures. *Must be a prank,* he thought. *Someone feeling nostalgic.*

He had watched the move again a few years ago on the demands of his younger nieces and nephews, but he'd found it a lot less scary than his thirteen-year-old self had remembered. The effects were cheesy, the story thin, and the ending cliché. The kids had enjoyed it, though, and drew little stick figures everywhere, just as he had.

Seeing the figure hanging in the tree brought the old creeping unease back again, though it didn't look much like the ones from the movie.

There was no sign of anyone around. He jumped up, yanked the figure out of the tree, and tossed it away, figuring that at least it wouldn't spook Evelyn or Zan as they came down the road. He had to wipe his hands off on his jeans several times before the oil-slick feeling faded.

The rain was coming down even harder and he was relieved to pull up safely between Evelyn's van and Zan's truck. He loped up the stairs and knocked on the door, glad of the overhang.

Zan peered around the open door, her dark eyes questioning. When she saw it was Shawn, she opened the door properly.

"Hi," she said.

"Hi," he answered, trying for jovial, but unsure he was pulling it off. The rain pounded on the overhanging roof, and he still felt dirty. "I was hoping to talk to you guys."

Zan pursed her lips but moved out of the way to admit him, dripping a little, into the foyer. "Evelyn!" she called, but frowned when there was no response. "She might still be in bed. I was just putting on the coffee."

Shawn winced, feeling like a heel for not bringing anything with him. Searching for Lori the evening before and then spending half the night trying various ways to contact her had driven out all semblance of manners. His *Nts T'its* would have tapped his head with a spoon.

"Would you prefer me to wait outside?" he asked.

Zan smiled a little. "I think I can take you if you try something," she said, and although her tone was joking, Shawn was pretty sure she probably could. In her bare feet, she was still an inch taller than him, and her arms looked strong. He grinned at her and followed her into the kitchen.

The gray outside made the kitchen seem brighter and warmer than usual and the smell of coffee was the perfect way to defeat the wet smell of his clothes. He sat down at the chair she gestured him to and a moment later there was a chipped mug in front of him.

"Quiet night?" he asked, uncertain of what else to say.

Zan frowned. "Mostly," she said. "This place takes some getting used to after Coquitlam. It's *too* quiet, you know?"

"I went to school in Toronto," he said. "It took me weeks to get used to all the noise and lights and then when I came back here, it took another few weeks to get used to the quiet. I kept worrying I was going deaf."

Zan grinned. "I think I could get used to it, but then I also think I'd miss the coffee shops and restaurants."

"There's restaurants here," Shawn said. Zan cocked an eyebrow at him. "In Prince Rupert," he finished, and she dramatically rolled her eyes.

Shawn knew he looked tired, but when Evelyn came into the kitchen, wrapped in a dark blue bathrobe, he had to reevaluate his own sleepiness. Evelyn's hair was badly tousled, she had massive circles under her eyes, and her skin had the waxy look of someone who worked night shifts for two weeks and still wasn't used to it. Her shoulders were slumped, and she kept flinching at the growls of thunder.

"Coffee," Zan said, thrusting her the large mug that she had just poured for herself. "You look terrible."

Evelyn mumbled something and then refocused on Shawn and looked horrified.

"I've seen far worse," he quickly reassured her. "You have kids, you're in a new place. I'm shocked you're not more tired." Though privately, he wasn't sure it was possible to look *more* tired than Evelyn did, and still remain upright.

Evelyn didn't look mollified, but she was far more interested in drinking coffee than pursuing the matter.

"What are you doing here?" she asked a few minutes later and then looked faintly ashamed of her rudeness.

Shawn took no offense. "I need to talk to you, but it can wait until you're more awake."

"I don't think I'll be getting any more awake," she grumbled, but she got up and came back several minutes later in actual clothing with her hair pulled back. By that point, Zan had poured her own coffee and taken the seat between them. Evelyn topped up her mug and sat down. "How can we help you?"

"I was wondering if you'd seen a woman around here. A few inches shorter than me, black hair, dark eyes, probably dressed in beat up leggings and a hoodie. She's about five years younger than me. Her name's Lori."

"I haven't seen anyone like that around here," Evelyn said, looking more awake. "No one has been up here other than you and Zan. And Kal of course."

Zan shook her head. "I didn't see anyone like that when I was driving in. Has she been missing for long?"

"I don't know," Shawn said uncertainly. "Lori is my cousin and she's... she's not good at taking care of herself. She parties and gets into trouble with her so-called friends. She left a weird Facebook status the other day and no one has seen her in a couple of days. I thought maybe she was just hanging around sulking – she just dumped her boyfriend, or so she said – but she's not in any of her usual spots." He realized he was babbling and clamped his mouth shut.

"I'm sorry," Evelyn said and Zan shook her head. "I know what it's like to have someone who doesn't take care of themselves around."

"Yeah," Zan said darkly. "Me too."

Shawn frowned, but he left it alone.

"We'll keep an eye out for her," Evelyn said. "Maybe she'll wander here."

"I hope so," Shawn said. "Though better still if she wanders back home."

"Have the police been called?" Evelyn asked.

Zan and Shawn both snorted at the same time.

"What?"

"Police out this way aren't much use," Shawn said. "Oh, they'll say they'll look into it, but the few who are decent are stretched too thin and the rest will mutter about drunk Indians and file it under DC."

"DC?"

"Don't Care," Zan answered.

"Oh," Evelyn said, looking down at the table.

"Everyone in Port Edward knows she's disappeared," Shawn said. "We're all looking. If no one turns anything up today, we'll file a report in Prince Rupert, for all the good it'll do."

They all sat in slightly awkward silence for a minute, but before it could mount too high, the quiet was broken by Christopher and Simon coming in, arguing about the rain and what to do for the day. Simon wasn't putting nearly as much energy into the fight as usual, with the result that Evelyn figured they would be playing Hide and Seek and then Mario.

"Good morning," Shawn said, trying to lighten the atmosphere. Christopher looked pleased to see him, but Simon looked away and busied himself with the toaster.

"You came in the storm to see us?" Christopher asked, slightly wide eyed as a bolt of lightning lit up the kitchen.

"And why not?" Shawn said, grinning.

Christopher smiled back, but Simon huffed a slight sigh.

"Although I should get back to Prince Rupert and get some work done," Shawn said, draining the last of his coffee as the storm settled to rain and the last of the thunder grumbled away. "Thanks for keeping an eye out for me."

"I'll let you know if she turns up," Evelyn said, and he nodded and saw himself out.

"If who shows up?" Simon asked.

"One of Shawn's cousins," Evelyn answered. "A woman. Have you seen anyone who looks a bit like Shawn?"

Simon looked uncomfortable and Evelyn managed the trick of looking at him without staring directly at him. Zan wished she could learn that one for clients, but it seemed to be a skill reserved for parents.

"That dream I had last night," he said. "Remember? I told you there was someone outside?"

Zan and Evelyn exchanged looks. "But there was no sign of anyone," Evelyn said gently.

"I know," Simon said. "But still."

Zan stretched and stood up. "Let's take a closer look outside," she suggested. "No one should be out in the rain, lost, confused and cold. Maybe Simon did see her through the window or something."

Evelyn nodded. "All right. You boys stay on the back porch while we look."

The two women pulled on their jackets and headed out. The storm had subsided, but the rain was still coming down, creating puddles in the grass. Small waterfalls came from the gutters, and the greenhouse looked miserable and gray.

"She was in the middle of the yard," Simon said. "She was by the trees at first, but then she came closer."

Zan nodded and the two women spread out, trying to see any sign of another person. It was hard to see much in the rain and dim light, but they gave it their best shot. Even when the greenhouse door opened to let Kal out, they barely paused.

Though when Kal hailed them, they had little choice but to stop.

"What are you looking for?" he asked Evelyn, giving Zan a puzzled look.

"Oh," Evelyn said, pushing her hood back so that she could look up at him. "Sorry. A friend from Port Edward was asking if we had seen his cousin around here and my son thought he saw her last night so we're looking for any sign of her."

Kal nodded, but his light hazel eyes were still studying Zan.

"And that's Zandra," Evelyn added. "She's my friend from Coquitlam and she came to stay for a bit."

Zan met Kal's gaze straight on, offering her hand for him to shake. He gave it a confused look for a fleeting moment and then took it. "A pleasure," he said. "My name is Kal."

"You're the gardener Evelyn mentioned," Zan said.

Kal's teeth showed in a brief smile while Zan shook his hand and then she hissed out a breath as a spark of static danced around her fingers.

"Sorry," he said immediately as she backed away, shaking her hand.

"Some people are like that," Zan said, but she looked a little suspicious.

"I haven't seen anyone on the grounds other than you and Shawn," Kal said, turning his attention back to Evelyn. "And no sign that anyone was here last night."

"He may have dreamed it," Evelyn said, sounding apologetic without really knowing why. Kal frowned at her.

"I didn't mean that he *didn't* see what he said he saw," he said mildly. "Only that there have been no signs. And that in itself may be peculiar. Still, good luck and I hope that the cousin is well." He nodded to Zan and returned to the greenhouse, coming out a moment later with a weed whacker and a determined stride for the parking area, despite the rain.

"Does he zap everyone?" Zan asked, still shaking some of the pins and needles out of her fingers.

"Yeah."

Zan's eyes narrowed. "He seems... nice?"

"Weird is the word you're looking for," Evelyn said firmly. "He scares me. I'd fire him except I have no idea what to do with the grounds."

They searched around some more, but the rain started coming down harder than ever and even Kal admitted defeat on his work when the storm circled back around with a crack of thunder. Weird or not, he was still soaked and shivering a little, compelling Evelyn to invite him inside to dry off before he returned to town.

The boys were upstairs, but the three adults huddled around the kitchen table, each mentally urging the coffee machine on to greater speeds. Zan was studying Kal out of the corner of her eye, but he was leaning back in his chair, eyes half-closed, looking at the ceiling. Evelyn managed to hold in a shudder – the boys were in the room just above them and it felt like Kal was watching them play.

"Do you have family in town?" Zan finally asked, breaking the slightly tense quiet.

"No," Kal said, pinning his hazel eyes on her. "We parted ways a long time ago. I haven't spoken to them since."

"No partner?"

"No," Kal said. He didn't seem upset about it. "No children either. I like children though. They are innocent and yet fierce." He contemplated the coffee Evelyn was pouring. "I have found that many people lose that complexity over time."

The two women exchanged uneasy looks and Kal smiled a little. "As I told Evelyn before," he said, his tone gentle. "I will not harm anyone here. There's nothing to fear from me."

Zan was about to respond – she wasn't sure *how*, but that had never stopped her before – when there was a bang from upstairs.

"The boys, probably," Evelyn said.

"It didn't come from their rooms," Zan answered, and Evelyn gripped the counter. There was another bang and even Kal looked uneasy.

"Let's just go check," Zan urged, and Evelyn led the way upstairs.

Both the boys were peering around the doorway of Simon's room. Christopher looked nervous.

"Was that you?" Evelyn asked.

They both shook their heads and opened the door wider to reveal that they had probably been reading, judging from the discarded books.

"It came from the attic," Christopher said, and Simon rolled his eyes.

"It came from outside," he argued.

"Boys," Evelyn said, and they quieted.

"Whatever it was, it seems to have stopped," Zan said. "Maybe it was outside. Might have been a bird that lost its way."

They waited for a couple of minutes, but the house was quiet again. Kal was the first to shake off the unease and went back downstairs with the women following him.

It was a tense several minutes while Kal finished his coffee. Once he left, Evelyn felt herself give a sigh of relief.

"He's a little ominous," Zan said. "But then, this whole house is spooky."

"Yeah," Evelyn said, taking their mugs to the sink.

If anything, the rain was getting even heavier. Small creeks wound their way through the grass and streamed down the driveway. The vehicles outside were shining in the light thrown off from the porch and the clouds were heavy. There was the sound Simon reading Christopher passages of a books, but otherwise the house as silent. It was almost hypnotic and Evelyn had to start herself out of a reverie that wiped out ten minutes before she realized it.

"I guess we can paint today," Zan said, also yanking herself out of watching the rain slide down the window. "It's pretty nasty out there."

Evelyn shrugged. Moving out of her chair felt like more effort than it was worth, and judging from how Zan was back to staring out the window, she felt the same way.

***

"Mom?"

The voice barely penetrated the thick fog in Evelyn's head.

"Mom!"

"What?" she asked dreamily. There had been a man's voice murmuring stories. Now there was someone shaking her shoulder.

The light outside had changed. The rain was reduced to a drizzle and the clouds were thinning, letting weak beams of sunlight through. Zan was staring out the window as well, but when Christopher clambered into her lap, she seemed to snap awake.

"Mom!"

Evelyn shook herself hard. "I'm sorry, Simon," she said. Her eyes slid over to the clock on the stove. It was past lunch.

"Were you asleep?" Simon asked. "You and aunt Zan have been sitting here for *hours.*"

"I... I guess so," Evelyn said, now feeling alarmed. The man's murmurs disappeared. "I guess none of us slept very well last night." She tried a smile for her son, but it must have looked as ghastly as she felt since Simon wrinkled his nose and didn't look reassured.

Zan shook her head. "What the hell?" she complained. "How did most of the morning go without us noticing?"

Evelyn still felt like she wanted to sink back into lethargy and find the man murmuring stories to her, but Simon was staring worriedly at her, and Christopher was pulling on Zan's hand. "I'm hungry," he said.

Getting out of her chair was one of the hardest things Evelyn had done in a while, but she managed it and as she did, she suddenly felt energy spike through her. "I guess we needed a nap," she said, trying for levity, but Zan didn't seem to be buying it. She also dragged herself out of her chair, but once back on her feet, resumed her usual smiles and bounce.

The boys were worried, but they ate their lunch of macaroni and, by the end of it, seemed to have decided it was just an Adult Thing. Besides, the rain had stopped, and they both wanted to go outside: Christopher to stomp in puddles and Simon to investigate worms. Evelyn gave the chairs an uneasy look and followed them. Zan was shaking off the last of her lethargy with a shower.

After the rain, under the gently brightening sky, the house seemed to glow. The boys were happily playing in the front yard. Evelyn leaned against her SUV, studying the building. The outside paint needed to be brightened up, of course, and a few things needed to be fixed, but the house didn't really seem frightening anymore. In fact, it felt welcome, comforting. Shabby to be sure, but in a cozy way. She could *feel* her uncle's presence more strongly than before, and it gave her a sense of peace.

Maybe we could just stay here forever.

Chapter Twelve

Two days passed with no sign of Lori.

Liz had no choice but to call the police and while they canvassed the village and the nearby wilderness, Shawn knew deep down that she wouldn't be found. Social media lit up with requests for information from as far as Edmonton where a few far-flung family members lived, but nothing more than well wishes returned.

As time passed, Shawn's feelings of dread increased. Lori had never gone farther than Terrace in her life and never expressed an interest in leaving. Port Edward was all she knew, all she *wanted* to know. She'd been one of the loudest naysayers when he'd gone to school out east. He knew it was mostly based on fear, but it was all the more powerful for that.

The police though were sure that she had left the village under her own power and would communicate if and when she was ready to. Aaron snorted in annoyance, but was unsurprised.

"This is what they always say," he told his son. "We just have to hope that this one time they're right, for Liz's sake."

Shawn kept a positive outlook around his aunt, who was already mentally fragile after helping his grandmother smudge the old house in the hills, but privately he harboured the horrible thought that something had killed Lori on one of her drunken ramblings. Maybe a cougar had come down from the hills or she'd angered a bear.

The stick figure of bones he'd found in the forest hung in his mind's eye and he shivered.

The police did talk to Evelyn, but there had been no sign of Lori there and Simon was positive now that he had dreamed seeing a woman in the middle of the night, so that was another dead end. They had even questioned Kal, but according to the local gossip at the bar, the man was a pleasant stone wall.

"He's from out east," one woman said in a tone that meant this explained everything from Kal's personality to his hair.

Shawn thought it was dubious Kal had anything to do with it anyway. The gardener had been employed by Jason and he showed no sign of wanting to do anything other than his job. Murdering women seemed outside the purview of someone who dedicated his energy to plants.

But it would be foolish to *completely* discount him, so Shawn kept an eye on him when he came into the village or Prince Rupert for supplies.

"What do you think of him?" he asked his father over their paperwork. Aaron raised an eyebrow.

"Kal? Nothing. I assume he was hired by Jason about the time he was dying. I think he's from Terrace, or at least lives there. He must be a hard worker and know what he's doing, or he wouldn't have stuck around. And I guess Evelyn must agree since she kept him on." He frowned. "You don't think he's got anything to do with Lori's disappearance?"

"Just trying to figure it out," Shawn sighed.

"I didn't want to say anything to Liz, but it was probably something natural," Aaron sighed. "She hasn't been doing well, weird Facebook posts aside."

But it's the sixth or seventh disappearance in the past few years, Shawn mentally argued. Not the same MO as the others who had vanished close to Evelyn's house, but *still*. Weird. And if Kal had been living in Terrace, and knew the area, he could have been around for all of them. Why else take up work in the middle of nowhere?

Maybe he should check on Evelyn again. And maybe it was time to convince her to sell.

***

Simon had decided to look for the missing woman.

He *told* the police that he had dreamed seeing her, but that was only because he didn't know how else to explain what he'd seen. It sounded stupid in his own mind, and he still felt like maybe it hadn't been her, or it had been her, but she'd run off. Either way, the police probably wouldn't help much. They had basically patted his head and ignored him, so he didn't have much faith in their ability to pay attention to anything he said.

The police hadn't done much to keep him and his brother safe from his father's drinking after all. Even after the accident, they had taken his dad away, but he was let go soon after and right back to drinking.

And he knew that they were jerks to people like Shawn. He *liked* Shawn.

No, Simon had no faith in the police to find the woman, but she had come to him, and she might do it again if he was far enough away from the house. So, one early morning the day after the police came to ask questions, he packed himself some food, plenty of water, and a few bandages in case she was hurt, and then headed off into the woods, the stick figure he found a warm and reassuring weight in his pocket. It gave him the feeling that he was doing the Right Thing.

Sunlight seeped through the branches of the cedars and spruce trees, tracing dust motes and thin deer trails. It smelled of sap and sharp needles, the air cool in the shadows. There was the whine of a few early morning mosquitoes, but otherwise, it was quiet.

"I won't go too far," Simon said aloud. He didn't want to get lost out here like the woman after all, and he was worried about bears and moose. Christopher was a dope for wanting to see them; Simon knew full well they could kill him. "But if you're out here, strange woman, I'm here to help you. I think Shawn might be looking for you too."

He figured that he would be quite the hero if he could just *find* her. She had disappeared from the back yard, but she couldn't have run across it since there had been no footprints, so she must have gone around the paved side and back into the woods. There were all kinds of places she could have gotten lost.

He had plenty of food and water and was ready to save the day.

***

When Evelyn came down to make breakfast, she didn't think much of the fact that only Christopher and Zan came down to eat it. Simon had been sleeping in more of late and she wasn't going to drag him out of bed to be surly when he was perfectly capable of getting his own food. But as the morning wore on, she began to have the uneasy feeling that something was amiss and when she noticed his shoes and coat were gone, the feeling coalesced into a spiked stone in her stomach.

"Christopher, did Simon say anything to you about going out this morning?"

"No," he said. "I didn't see him."

Zan's eyes were wide, and she shook her head.

"I'm sure he's fine," she said. "You said yourself that he's been outside a lot exploring. Maybe he saw an animal and went after it. We'll just go out and find him."

"Right," Evelyn said and allowed her friend to lead her to the front door to get their coats and shoes and hold Christopher back from running off. The sun was still shining on them, but it seemed oddly thin, wisps of cloud dimming its light and creating a chill. There was a very clear trail leading into the woods in the still-damp grass.

"Let's go," Evelyn said firmly, holding her youngest son's hand while Zan held the other one. "We'll find him. He left a pretty clear trail of footprints to follow."

None of them noticed the greenhouse door ease open and a shadow slip out after them as they plunged into the trees. The raven that harshly called after their passage made Zan nearly jump out of her skin.

***

The sunlight was bright enough now to banish uneasy feelings as Shawn made his way back to the house. His night had been restless, punctuated by memories of Lori and the strange gardener. By the time dawn crept over the mountains, he was sure that Kal had something to do with her disappearance and he was going to prove it.

Of course, the first thing he had to do was get back there, warn Evelyn, and make sure everyone was all right.

He was relieved when he pulled into the driveway to see no sign of anyone outside, but both vehicles were there. He loped up the stairs and knocked on the door. It cracked open under his knuckles and he peered into the dim room beyond.

"Evelyn?" he called. "Zan? Anyone home?"

Only silence yawned at him. He braced himself and went inside, checking every room, but there was no sign of women or boys, though they clearly *had* been home, judging from the breakfast dishes in the sink. He crossed his arms over his chest and shivered in spite of the warm sunshine beating through the window.

There was something else in the house with him. He could *feel* it.

Shawn carefully walked to the back door. He felt a particular aversion to the basement and door and turned his back on it, barely daring to breathe, until he got to the back porch. He scowled at the clouds beginning to pile up on the horizon and then squinted a little, noticing that the greenhouse door was hanging open and there were impressions in the grass leading to the forest.

"Shit," he said.

He didn't know *why* they had gone into the woods, but he didn't have a good feeling about it. "Simon," he said aloud. "They're probably looking for him."

But there was no reason for the family to have left their greenhouse door wide open and Kal wouldn't have done it either, assuming he was who he said he was, so someone or something else must have been here. And now that he was outside, he didn't know why the house behind him still felt as though it was looming over him. He'd never felt that way about it before.

Listen to your ancestors.

He was listening, but so far all his instincts were doing were screaming at him to not go back into the house. Instead, he strode towards the greenhouse, the ground still saturated with the night's rain, sucking at his feet. He could shut that door at least before a bear got in, and then decide what to do next. There was no point in going into the trees after them or they might all be lost, but he could wait for a bit, try to get some cell service, and call the police if they stayed missing for too long.

He easily closed the door and then wasn't sure what to do. The house glared from behind him, the forest clawed at the corners of his eyes, and the skies were beginning to turn gray. He thought he would do a circuit of the perimeter of the greenhouse to look for any sign of Simon or Kal, and then check back at the house in the dim hope that they might have returned through the front door. He started his trek, studiously avoiding looking at the house or the trees and sky, which mostly left him looking at the ground.

Behind the greenhouse, the earth was even softer and muddier. It looked as though it had been freshly churned up and he wondered if Kal had been doing work or maybe the boys had been playing in it. Imagining Christopher making mud pies helped keep his mind off the trees.

Then he noticed a gleam of silver.

A ring.

Still attached to a finger. And he knew damn well whose ring that was.

"Lori," he choked in horror, falling backwards on his butt and pushing himself away.

***

The rain was just starting to fall, but with so many trees, only a few drops came through. It was colder beneath the branches, which smacked wetly against them. The smell of greenery was strong, mingling with the scent of damp earth. Christopher looked miserable.

"Simon!" Zan called, her voice bouncing off the trees and echoing eerily back to them. She exchanged glances with Evelyn and they both shivered.

There was a path through the forest, and they stuck with it as though the trees were walls. Even Christopher didn't stray to look at wet moss or shrubs; he stuck close to Evelyn, his dark eyes wide.

Zan looked around, trying to see through the trees as much as she could, but there was no sign of Simon. However, she did see another of the bone figures hanging from a tree, its threads soaked with water, the once-white bones now gray. She shuddered and steered Evelyn away from any possible chance of seeing the macabre object. Fortunately, Evelyn was so intent on finding her son that she wasn't paying attention to much else. Zan's gaze kept sliding to the figure until it disappeared from her view.

Then she saw another one. And *another one*. They were beginning to cluster and, in those numbers, they rattled in the light breeze.

It was impossible to hide them from Evelyn now.

"What are those?" Evelyn asked, stopping dead, and staring at the weird figures.

"Probably something that someone from Port Edward did up," Zan said. "A game maybe. Nothing to worry about, I'm sure."

Evelyn tilted her head at them and, to Zan's faint horror, Christopher mirrored her. "They look... familiar."

Zan tried to laugh, but it was hollow. "Remember The Blair Witch Project back when we were kids? That's probably what you're thinking of."

"Those were made from sticks," Evelyn said. "Are those... bone?"

Zan felt as though her spine was trying to crawl into her stomach. "I don't know," she fibbed. "We're here to find Simon, though, remember?"

Evelyn nodded and, to Zan's relief, came back to herself. "I know," she said, tearing her eyes away from the dangling figures. "Let's go. He can't have gotten much farther than this."

Christopher buried his face in Evelyn's hip and Zan had to pick him up to keep them moving. They both firmly ignored the fact that the number of bone figures hanging in the trees was growing.

The path ended in a small clearing and the two women stopped at the edge, paralyzed by what they saw.

There was a bundle of cloth and limbs lying sprawled in the clearing which was clearly Simon. Something was looming over him, impressions of arms encircling his body and holding his face up in a horrible parody of giving the breath of life.

Then something golden *smashed* into the shadowy figure and sent it sprawling into the trees. A cacophony of raven shrieks split the air, outraged perhaps at the intrusion into their homes. Evelyn's paralysis broke at that, and she ran forward to take her son into her arms. Zan held on to Christopher, her eyes desperately trying to see something of the fight that was happening in the trees, but all she saw were flashes of shadow and gold, whipping around each other.

Simon looked as though he was asleep and there were no injuries, but despite calling his name several times and shaking him, he wouldn't wake up. His face looked strangely pale and the rain falling on him didn't even make him twitch.

The weird golden glow and the shadow retreated deeper into the trees, the ravens quieted, and Zan carefully put Christopher down and joined Evelyn.

"We have to get him back home," Evelyn said. "He won't wake up! Something must have happened to him. Can we get him to a hospital?"

Zan was about to say that she would drive him to Prince Rupert, Terrace, or even Prince George if that's what it took when there was a crashing sound behind them. She shrieked and lunged to stand in front of Evelyn, shoving Christopher behind her, but the crashing simply resolved itself to be two men in uniform who looked as startled as the women were.

"Evelyn Brody?" the older cop asked. "What's going on?"

"What are you doing here?" Zan asked.

"My son needs help," Evelyn said. "He wandered out here and collapsed."

Christopher scowled at the police, but then hid behind his mother when the younger one smiled at him. The cop then went to check on Simon and his older partner looked over Zan and Evelyn. "We need to get back to the house. We can take your boy to the hospital."

"Why are you here?" Zan asked again. "Not that I'm not grateful, it was good timing, but..."

The older man fiddled a bit with his holster. "We were called out to your property by Shawn Myers. A body was found on your grounds."

"A body?" Evelyn repeated, her face pale with tinges of green. "But... *who? How?*"

"We're in the process of exhuming her," the officer said. "Shawn told us you were in the forest looking for your son."

"Yes," Zan said. The younger officer finished his check over Simon and shrugged.

"Do you mind if one of us carries your son back to the house?" the older man asked gently. "There's nothing that can be done out here for him."

"Of course not," Evelyn said, still looking sick.

Christopher began to cry, and Evelyn wrapped her arms around him as the officer picked Simon up and began to carry him back to the house. Zan helped Christopher stagger home. Evelyn felt as though everything around was muffled and far away.

What happened to my son? And what was that... thing... standing over him?

Chapter Thirteen

Hospitals were all the same. Having spent quite a bit of time in them over the past several months, Evelyn felt quite secure in her opinion.

The waiting room was too cool and a shade too bright. The sounds were too sharp and sudden, and the ticking of the clock spelled out both the strain of hope and shattering into reality. The less often she heard from the doctor, the more she could simultaneously convince herself that they were working hard to restore her son and that all hope was lost.

Fear was the smell of antiseptic in the air, sharp and invasive.

Zan stayed back at the house with Christopher, but Shawn promised to check in with them, bobbing between the house and the hospital in Prince Rupert like a worried and deflated balloon. He didn't say much when he did come, but he forced coffee and fry bread on her, and talked quietly to the nurse at the front station who seemed to know him. There was never anything to add, though.

The remorseless ticking of the clock reminded everyone how brief mortal life was.

A nurse finally came into the waiting room and pulled Evelyn into a hospital room where her son lay on the bed, looking shrunken against the sheets. His clothing was neatly folded on the side, but otherwise, there were no personal touches in the room. The doctor tucked him in a little more and turned to face Evelyn.

"Does your son have anything in his medical history that we should know about?" he asked. "Brain tumour? Heart problems? Seizures?"

"No," Evelyn said. "He's always been healthy. And nothing like that runs in my family, as far as I know."

"He's displaying the signs of having had a stroke," the doctor said. "Have you noticed any change in behaviours the past few days? More sleepy than usual or trouble speaking? Did he complain about headaches or dizziness?"

Evelyn combed her fingers through her hair. "He was sleeping more, but I thought it was just, you know, teenage behaviour. He didn't complain about headaches or anything like that." She wasn't sure how to tell him that Simon had become weirdly obsessed with living at the house or his ventures into the forest. "He was in the woods when we found him."

"There's no sign of injury," the older man hastened to reassure her. The harsh lights from the hall glinted a little on his bald head. "Whatever happened, it's all internal. We're going to run more tests." He gave her a sympathetic pat on the shoulder. "Primarily, we want to run a CT scan and an EEG to look for injuries or abnormal brain activity. That will help us pin down what happened. But we need your consent and we're planning to move him to Terrace as soon as possible. They have the equipment to do the EEG and any other tests."

The next half hour was a blur as the doctor explained the processes and Evelyn signed forms. When she was released from his office, she felt wrung out and was relieved to see Shawn idling in the waiting room.

"Sherri thinks it will take a few hours for everything to be done here so they won't transfer him until tomorrow," he said. "You should get some rest and actual food. I can drive you back home."

She felt like she shouldn't want to go anywhere, but there was a powerful need to walk through the house doors, look out at the greenhouse, and even go into the basement and make sure nothing had changed in her absence. She nodded and Shawn helped her out to his jeep, looking worried.

"The doctors are amazing in Terrace," he said, trying to fill the ballooning silence as they drove. "I'm sure Simon will be fine."

"I must have missed something," Evelyn said dully. "Maybe he just didn't want to tell me that he was having headaches or feeling dizzy."

There wasn't much Shawn could say to that, but he patted her hand and whipped through Prince Rupert and over the bridge back to the mainland and home.

It was past supper, and the house still hosted a few police officers. Shawn folded his arms over his chest and huffed out a breath as Evelyn stared at them. They were mostly concentrated in her backyard, judging from the sounds of talking, but there was one officer stationed at her front door.

"I'm sorry," she said immediately. "I... well, I mean, I didn't *forget*, obviously, but..."

"It's fine," Shawn said. "You had other pressing things in mind, and I've already been in and out. They removed the body."

"Was it someone you knew?" Evelyn asked.

"Yeah," Shawn said heavily.

Evelyn took her turn to pat his shoulder. "She was the woman you were looking for, wasn't she?"

"My cousin Lori," Shawn said. "Dad had to do a positive ID on her." His dad had looked haunted afterwards and refused to discuss what condition his cousin had been in. Shawn had not had the opportunity to look for himself; once the police were summoned, she had been quickly removed and taken to Prince Rupert for the autopsy.

Evelyn felt sick all over again.

"They're going to want to question you," Shawn warned. "They already talked to Zan."

"Does your father do cases like this?" Evelyn asked vaguely and Shawn shook his head.

"Civil lawyer, not criminal. But I'll ask around, if you like."

"Thanks," Evelyn said. "Not that... I mean, *I* didn't..."

Shawn rubbed her shoulder a little. "I know you didn't, and I know Zan didn't either," he said firmly. "But just in case."

The officer at the door saw them coming and ushered them both inside. Zan was playing on the floor of the living room with Christopher, but the boy launched himself at his mom as soon as they came in.

"Where's Simon?" he demanded.

"Still at the hospital," Evelyn said, crouching down and hugging her youngest son close. He still smelled of outdoors and had grubby knees. Somehow, excruciatingly, it was still the same day. "They are working on fixing him, but he's going to Terrace tomorrow."

"Are we going to Terrace too?" Christopher asked.

"Of course we are," Evelyn said. She looked over his head at Zan who chewed her lip a little and jerked her head in the direction of the backyard. Evelyn reluctantly released her boy and made her way to the back of the house.

The yard had several officers milling around. A few of them looked as though they were simply waiting, but she could see the shadows of at least two others behind the greenhouse, which had been cordoned off with yellow police tape. *Kal isn't going to be happy,* she thought irrelevantly and then wondered where he was.

"Was Kal not here today?" she asked aloud.

"I didn't see him, but I only stopped in a couple of times to update Zan."

"I didn't see him today," Zan said, narrowing her eyes slightly.

It was odd, but maybe he didn't bother to come because word had spread about the body found in the yard and he figured he wouldn't be able to work anyway. Port Edward was a small community after all, and a body found in a yard was good gossip fodder. Perhaps he had stopped for something at the new bakery, heard the news, and returned to... wherever he lived.

Still, red flags rose in Evelyn's mind.

One of the officers spotted her and came over, gesturing for her to go back into the kitchen with him. He was a middle-aged man with graying brown hair and friendly enough features, though his eyes were chips of slate as he studied the house and her.

"Ms. Brody," he said with little preamble. "You're the owner of this house?"

"Yes."

"And is this everyone who lives here?" He gestured around at Zan and Shawn.

"Shawn doesn't live here," Evelyn said immediately, and Shawn shook his head in agreement. "And my oldest son is in the hospital."

"My condolences," the officer said, but he didn't sound terribly sympathetic or surprised to hear it.

"Zan doesn't live here either, but she's visiting," Evelyn said. "And there's a gardener named Kal, but I don't know if he came in today."

The officer gave her a sharp look. "Is that usual? Is today his day off?"

Feeling strangely flustered, Evelyn floundered for a moment. "Well, no," she said. "I mean, I don't... I'm not sure when his days off are. He was employed by my uncle before he died, and I'm letting him work here until I sell the house. I assume he heard what happened and figured he wouldn't be able to work anyway, so why make the trip." She realized this sounded a bit lame since he should have called her at least, but she wasn't sure what else to say.

"Do you know where he lives?"

"Port Edward maybe?" she said, feeling stupider by the moment. "I'm sorry. I don't really know a lot about him. I don't even know his last name. It was all arranged by my uncle and I'm not intending to keep the place. He can't live too far away since he comes early in the morning to work."

The officer hmmed a little, but he scribbled in his notebook. "Anyone else with access to the house?"

Evelyn weakly shrugged. "It's not as though this place has a fence around it," she said. "I guess anyone in Port Edward or Prince Rupert could get up here easily enough. I haven't seen anyone around I didn't recognize."

"Have you ever met the deceased? She's a young Indigenous woman."

Evelyn shook her head. "All I know about is that Shawn was looking for her and I haven't seen anyone like that around here."

"What was your son doing out in the woods?"

"He likes exploring out there," Evelyn said, her stomach slowly crawling up her throat. "He looks for bugs, mushrooms, plants, and other things. We went looking for him when he didn't come for breakfast and I noticed his shoes were gone."

"And you said he's now in the hospital?"

"He collapsed out there," Evelyn said. "We don't know what happened yet."

"Any sign of injury?"

"*No*," Evelyn said, nauseated.

The officer scribbled a few more notes and then closed the notebook with a snap. To Evelyn's strained nerves, it sounded like a bone breaking.

"I assume you won't be going anywhere in the next few days," he said, making it sound like a threat.

"I have to go to Terrace if they move my son," she whispered. Shawn was now standing behind the officer, scowling at him.

"Be sure to inform the precinct if you do go to Terrace," the officer said.

Evelyn bobbed her head.

"I'd appreciate you keeping my family in the loop as well," Shawn said coolly as he walked by the officer to stand by Evelyn. "Lori is my cousin."

"Her mother will be kept informed."

"As will my dad," Shawn said firmly. "My aunt is not always the most communicative and she will likely be with him anyway."

The two men stared daggers at each other, but the officer must have decided it wasn't worth the fight. He nodded brusquely and went back outside. Evelyn slumped in her chair.

"Cops," Shawn snorted.

"I can't believe she died in my yard," Evelyn said. "That's... I'm sorry again, Shawn."

Shawn sighed. "Not your fault."

Christopher leaned against her shins, hiding under the table, as the police came in and out and didn't peek out until they had all left. Evelyn didn't feel like eating, but Shawn put a frozen pizza in the oven anyway.

"My dad will keep them in line," he said, still glowering in the direction the police had gone in. "He's not a criminal lawyer, but he has friends who are and he's not afraid to pull favours."

"How do you think it happened?" Evelyn asked. She didn't want to think about it, let alone talk about it, but her mind kept circling back like a vulture.

Shawn shrugged. "I don't know if you're asking how she died as much as how she ended up half buried behind your greenhouse," he said. "And I don't know the answer to either. The autopsy will give some answers, but..."

"More questions than answers, I'm sure," Evelyn said. She patted Christopher's head, and he buried his face in her lap.

They sat in silence until the oven timer beeped and Shawn excused himself to go home while they ate.

Evelyn ate, but it was mechanical, and Christopher only picked at his food, looking near tears the entire time. She knew he wasn't going to sleep well, but routine had to be at least vaguely maintained, so she ushered him into a bath, read him three stories, and left the light on in his room.

Zan had retreated to her room too, almost limp with exhaustion.

Evelyn could finally make the rounds of the house. The need for it had been pressing down on her and she rationalized that maybe there was some clue in the house as to what happened to Simon or Lori. Maybe Simon had gotten into something that made him sick. Maybe there was an intruder who killed Lori.

Maybe she just felt like she needed to check on everything and make sure the house was still *hers.*

The main floor was normal. The plastic had been removed from the furniture and was already looking a bit worn from the boys. The kitchen was clean, or as clean as she could be bothered with, the main foyer and stairs creaked reassuringly at her.

Simon's room was empty and cool, his window cracked open. She closed it and tried not to look at the unused bed since it made her eyes well up. Her room was more appealing, but she had to do the rounds before staring at the ceiling all night, wondering if her son would be all right.

She avoided the attic.

But the basement called to her. It was something she had to check; if there had been an intruder, they may have lurked down there, luring Lori to the butcher room. Shudders crawled up her spine, but the urge to go down and *check, be sure*, was stronger.

She flicked the light switch on, brightening up the wooden staircase and casting a shaky pool of light on the basement floor. Once she was halfway down, she could see the door to the butcher room, resolutely closed at her sons' demands.

There was still no sign that anything had been disturbed, but she carried on down the stairs anyway until she got to the basement floor and could look around properly.

The layer of dust on the shrouded boxes and furniture was unmoved and she felt as though she could breathe easy. The usual jumble of boxes and old furniture met her eyes in the main room. A couple of spiders skittered away from her footfalls, but otherwise, all was quiet.

She realized that she hadn't yet looked around at the stuff left behind by her uncle. There were several boxes labelled books, paperwork and Xmas ornaments; a bedraggled artificial Christmas tree, and a couple of armchairs full of holes that drooled stuffing. The lightbulb in the middle of the ceiling cast the room in a weird yellow-white glow, throwing back shadows.

A few things were covered in old sheets: a dresser with several half-open drawers (empty, save for dust and webs), a heavy looking bookcase that was empty, and a huge mirror. It had likely been in the master bedroom at some point since it matched her bed, but it had been moved downstairs due to a long crack that bisected it. If Evelyn stood at the right angle to it, her reflection shattered: Picasso in glass.

It felt comforting to be around her uncle's old things, even if they were cast-offs from his life. She closed her eyes and breathed in the mixed smell of old cloth, old books, wood, and the slight must that was inevitable in a basement. She reached out and carefully touched the cracked mirror.

Her reflection was still shattered, but far from horrifying her, she felt as though it fit her perfectly and she could stare at the broken pieces of her face and neck forever. The harsh angles made her features seem to melt and blur, taking off the worries and stress and replacing them with something foggy, easier to look at. Her blue eyes didn't look fearful anymore and wrinkles were too instinct to make out.

But a broken mirror should still have thrown back her reflection. As she studied it more, she realized with growing horror that the reflection had brown eyes, straight black hair, and dark skin, arms dotted with tiny scars.

It wasn't *her* in the mirror anymore.

"Help me," the woman mouthed, and Evelyn shrieked and threw the sheet back over the mirror. She stared at it for a second as the cloth settled and then shook her head. She was exhausted; she must have imagined it.

The cloth twitched and the shape of a hand and a painfully skinny wrist pushed it out, reaching for Evelyn. She screamed and ran for the stairs, taking as wide a detour away from the butcher room door as she could.

Something banged on the other side of the door and she fled up the stairs, slamming the basement door behind her.

But she could still hear something knocking, almost politely, from within the butcher room. She pelted upstairs and lay in bed, exhausted, anxious, and listening to the intermittent knocking until long past midnight when whatever it was finally gave up, far too late for her to get any sleep.

Chapter Fourteen

Aaron and Shawn brooded over their morning coffee, unwilling to face a day at work. Liz sat between them with her face buried in her arms. She had been crying off and on all night, and had exhausted her tears. The only thing that had come out of her other than tears was blaming herself for Lori's death.

"It was the fault of whoever killed her," Aaron tried to tell her, but she was too far gone in her grief to listen.

Port Edward was quiet, grieving as well. Losing another young adult when three had disappeared less than a year ago was a blow on a fragile community. The body would not be released for at least a few more days, though the elders and members of Shawn's family were planning Lori's celebration of life.

Aaron pushed aside some of his sister's hair to see that she truly had fallen asleep. He sighed and tucked a blanket around her shoulders, gesturing for Shawn to meet him in the other room. They both sprawled on Liz's ancient armchairs, unwilling to move much.

"How's Evelyn?" Aaron finally asked.

"In shock," Shawn said. "Between this and Simon being taken to the hospital... I didn't want to leave her alone, but I don't think she wanted me to stay. Her friend Zan is there with her, at least. Have you heard from the police yet?"

Aaron's mouth puckered. "No," he said. "The last I heard, they were looking for the gardener who works at Evelyn's house. He seems to be their main suspect."

Shawn narrowed his eyes. "He's mine too," he admitted. "Though it was a bit stupid of him if it was him, to bury her in a shallow grave behind the damn greenhouse."

His father shrugged. "People do stupid things."

There was no denying that and Shawn *wanted* to think that Kal had something to do with it, but he still worried at the assumption like it was a bad piece of fish. He couldn't figure out who *else* could have killed his cousin. She had always been popular and well liked; that had been part of the problem causing her to party hard and drown her less-than-desirable home life in alcohol.

"I've retained Mara," his dad said. "Just in case. She owes me a favour and she's been looking for a reason to stick it to the chief of police ever since that incident with the trucker raping Thomas and getting off on a technicality. She said she'll represent Evelyn and Zan if things come to that."

"That should take a weight off her mind."

Shawn's phone bleeped and he looked at it to see a message from Evelyn:

Simon being taken to Terrace hospital today for an ECG. Hospital in Rupert still can't figure out why he's in a coma.

"Do you need me today, dad?"

"Probably not," Aaron said, glancing at Shawn's phone. "I'll be here all day making sure Liz eats and vaguely takes care of herself. Does Evelyn need you?"

"Simon is getting taken to Terrace. She might need my help."

Aaron raised his eyebrows. "Spending a lot of time with her lately," he said mildly, and Shawn felt heat rise in his cheeks.

"If you're going to Terrace anyway, you can pick up some stuff for the office," he added, watching Shawn twitch from embarrassment. "I'll do up a list."

"Sure dad," Shawn said hastily. "I'll get supper for everyone too."

Aaron smirked a little and though grief still hung heavy in the house, for a brief moment, there was a hint of sunlight to break through the clouds.

***

The medical bus made its swift and stately way down the highway between Prince Rupert and Terrace. There weren't many people on it, but the adolescent in a coma had to be rushed to Terrace as quickly as possible to make to his tests. The nurse on duty was warned that he had a weirdly restless night, though none of the monitors had picked up the movements the overnight nurse had sworn happened.

There were only three other people, and normally the bus probably wouldn't have gone at all but for the youth. There was an elder who had been waiting for more testing for her hip, a woman who was being sent on to Prince George for a round of chemotherapy, and an older man who had diabetes and wanted more care than Prince Rupert could handle at the moment. They talked quietly among themselves, mostly about the boy lying prone in the back. The elder woman had given him a grim look when he was wheeled aboard.

Storm clouds rolled over the sky, but this was nothing new. It was summer and storms were usual, barely remarked upon. It was only about an hour to Terrace and some rain was hardly going to disrupt the trip.

Though the sudden crack of thunder overhead did make everyone jump a little, and then laugh at each other. The windows darkened and quickly became smeared with rain. A bolt of lightning lit up the road ahead and the driver cursed a little under his breath; the light refracted off the wet road, causing shards of crystal to dance in front of him.

There was a howl from the back of the bus. The youth was thrashing against the restraints, bucking and tossing wildly. It took a moment for the nurse to realize that he was thrashing in time to the thunder. The elder hissed a little under her breath and hunched away from the boy.

"What's going on?" one of the patients shouted.

"Everything is under control," the nurse said hastily. The boy's face looked strange – pale, but blotchy on his cheeks and forehead, and his lips looked far too red for someone who had been in a coma for almost twenty-four hours.

A massive crack of thunder over the bus caused the other passengers to jump and swear. The driver was an old hat with the northern roads and barely flinched. He was too busy keeping a careful eye on the road, watching for oncoming traffic, wildlife spooked by the storm, and fallen branches. In weather like this, a power line could come down, and depending on where it was, it would be hard to see until it was too late.

The wipers were going as quickly as they could, and the heat was turned down to prevent condensation from forming on the windows. The driver ignored the noise coming from the back of the bus; he knew his job and the nurse knew hers and there was no point in saying anything when all his focus needed to be on keeping the bus on the road.

Clouds piled on even more thickly and the rain fell in sheets. The driver wasn't fazed yet; it was turning into a bad storm, but nothing he couldn't handle as long as he kept his wits about him.

The moaning coming from the back of the bus made that trickier than usual, though. And the other patients were muttering as well, casting worried looks between the driver and the coma patient. Still, he kept his focus on the road, minding the pools of water that would cause him to hydroplane if he wasn't careful.

There was another vivid bolt of lightning that cause anyone looking out the window to see green and white afterimages for a moment, the driver included. He assumed the mirage was simply lasting longer than usual when he saw a large and spindly figure on the road before him. He blinked furiously to clear his eyes, but it refused to leave. As the bus continued up the road, the figure grew larger and the driver was sure he could see eyes in the approximate place where a face should be, staring balefully at the vehicle.

The driver shouted a bit and then slammed on the brakes, skidding in the water on the road. The passengers shrieked and swore, the nurse grabbed the youth to hold him steady, and the driver desperately tried to keep control of the bus as they hydroplaned. He was forced to take his foot off the brake and fought with the steering wheel to hold the bus straight, hoping against hope to feel the tires make contact with the road. The anti-lock brakes weren't working the way they were supposed to, and he swore.

The spindly figure seemed to loom large and then it abruptly vanished, and the bus finally skidded to a stop, pointing out towards the river which was being peppered with massive rain drops.

For a moment, the only sound was the heavy breathing of the passengers, the nurse's voice, and the pattering of rain on the bus. There was another crack of thunder and one of the patients looked out the window, looking behind them now, to see the spindly figure standing in the road, still staring at them.

"Nurse!" the man shouted.

Gotta get us out of here, the driver thought and though his every instinct drove him to try to leave as fast as he could, he knew damn well that he had to carefully turn the bus around and that going too fast would cause them to hydroplane again. Trying to ignore the chattering and worry of the patients behind him, he eased the bus forward, back, and turned it until they were pointing in the right direction, and then hit the gas and headed towards Terrace, thankful that no other vehicles had been on the road.

The boy screamed and the nurse shouted. He was arching his back and his mouth was open in a rictus of fear and agony. The spindly figure seemed to be reaching out towards the bus as it beat a retreat towards Terrace.

The nurse grabbed a hypodermic needle, loaded it with a sedative, and dosed the boy. It would take almost fifteen minutes before the drug could do its work, but at least he wouldn't get any worse, and he would start to settle quickly.

Though even after he stopped thrashing, his muscles kept twitching.

"Shit," the driver said and even the elders didn't reprimand him.

Of the spindly figure there was no longer any sign, but the rain poured down even harder, and thunder shook the windows all the way to Terrace.

***

The storm thrashed against Terrace and Evelyn had not been able to make good time to reach the hospital. Thankfully, Christopher had stayed quiet the entire trip, entertained by Zan who was teaching him how to make cat's cradle on his fingers. Every bit of Evelyn pushed her to go faster, to be at the hospital when Simon arrived, but she reined herself in. She wouldn't be of any use to her son if they crashed into the hills on one side, or the river on the other. Thunder and lightning stretched out across the highway, drowning both Port Edward and Terrace in a deluge of rain, wind, and thick dark clouds.

"Terrible storm," the front reception at the hospital commented as Evelyn came in with Zan and Christopher, all three of them soaked just from the walk from the parking lot. "Can I help you?"

Evelyn told her they were there for Simon and was directed to his room.

The Mills Memorial was an aging hospital, a dusty white and brown, low-slung building with one tower and plenty of windows. There was work being done on a brand new and much larger hospital nearby. From the window, Evelyn could see the cranes and frames of the new building, but in this storm, all work had been halted. They were almost spooky in the dim light, though everyone she heard talking about it were very excited.

One of the doctors stopped her at the door and glanced at Christopher and Zan. Taking the hint, Zan took Christopher to get a snack while the doctor stood with Evelyn.

"Your son had a bad seizure on the way into Terrace," she said. "The nurse had to sedate him. Has he ever had seizures before?"

"No," Evelyn said, her stomach pumping acid up her throat. "Never. Is he all right?"

"He seems fine, but he's still unconscious," the doctor said. "We want to get him in for those tests as soon as possible. You can see him," she added. "But there won't be much to see."

Evelyn pushed by her anyway to look in the small, slightly run-down room where her oldest son lay on the bed. There was a single chair and on the other side, an IV pole that kept his body alive while his mind wandered. She sank into the chair and picked up his hand. It was warm, but limp.

"I'm sorry, baby," she said, tears spilling down her cheeks. "We never should have come here."

There was a knock at the door, and she looked up to see Shawn craning his head around the frame. He held out a steaming travel cup, but he didn't say anything. She couldn't seem to get out of the chair to retrieve it, so he came inside and pressed it into her free hand.

"Thank you," she whispered.

"No problem," he said, looking at Simon. "No change?"

"The doctor said he had a seizure," she said around the lump in her throat. "But they don't know why yet."

"Nothing new in Port Edward either," Shawn said. "At least, not anything anyone is talking about. I thought I'd stay in town for a bit. If you need me, just text."

She nodded and he patted her shoulder and left her to her vigil.

Chapter Fifteen

The police searched Port Edward, Prince Rupert, and Terrace for Kal, but no one recognized him beyond the occasional cashier who vaguely remembered a man of his description buying food. Suspicious, they fanned out the search, putting out social media posts and asking their own contacts for any information about the dark-haired gardener.

Nothing turned up and when one of the cops turned up a complete lack of employment agreements between Jason and Kal, Kal went from a person of interest to a suspect. The tension at the station in Prince Rupert ratcheted. It was suddenly more likely that there was murderer in the area.

***

The storm beat against Terrace all day and well into the night, raging above the hospital and downtown. Grimly, weather reporters predicted it may last well into the night and cause localized flooding and wind damage. The hospital had back-up generators, but it was still alarming to see lightning flare through sky and thunder that shook the building.

And Simon's seizures seemed to follow the rhythm of the storm, growing worse when it was overhead and receding as the clouds did, only to circle around again. Intellectually,

Evelyn knew she was being ridiculous, but she couldn't help spotting patterns. Every time he seized, she was gently pushed out of the room to wait outside where she had to fight to keep from beating her fists on the walls. Even sedating Simon did little to stop him from moving to a frenetic rhythm that only he could hear.

They wouldn't do any tests in such conditions and by evening she was told she should get some food and find a place to sleep for the night. It was dangerous to drive home, even if she wanted to.

Zan had that part handled. She had secured them a motel room and was playing video games with Christopher. Guilt filled Evelyn as she staggered into the room. She hadn't put much thought towards her youngest son while her oldest one bucked and thrashed.

"How's Simon?" Zan asked as Christopher ran into his mother's arms.

"They couldn't do the tests on him. He keeps having seizures and they're worried about the chance of a power outage."

"They'll take good care of him," Zan said. "Shawn was in and out as well, but he went back to Port Edward. He said he'll be back in the morning if you need him."

"Okay," Evelyn said, falling backwards onto the bed. Christopher clambered up beside her, his soft dark hair brushing her ear.

Zan put a plate of chow mein beside her, but she couldn't bring herself to sit up and eat. The smell of the hospital was still in her nostrils and she kept worrying that somehow she had left the oven on or done something that would make them come home to a wreckage.

Or that the police had found another body.

A weird wave of homesickness shuddered through her and then passed.

"Simon will be okay, right?" Christopher whispered in her ear, and she hugged him.

"Of course he will be."

***

The man stood outside the Mills Memorial Hospital, long coat brushing around his knees, keeping the lashing rain off his clothing. He was staring at a third storey window with peculiar intensity and didn't even shield his eyes when lightning scarred the sky above. The wind ripped at his coat, but he was immovable.

The wind hissed in his ears, cold, malicious, bearing knives of unseasonable frost, but he waved it away.

"Get thee behind me," he murmured, smiling slightly at the indulgence.

The wind hissed again, old words of poison, but he stood like a rock and it broke on him. Above, the clouds began to thin and brilliant colours showed through from a display of northern lights.

In the hospital, in a third storey room, a doctor worked to calm Simon's seizures, which had grown increasingly more violent. The boy was flushed and sweating, thrashing in his bed, and nearly ripping out his IV. The usual methods completely failed, and all the doctor and nurses could do was keep anything dangerous away from the youth.

Another nurse going on her break heard the noise from within the room and her heart ached for the poor boy. She scampered outside for a quick vape and looked up to see the northern lights breaking through the clouds.

Dancing green and purple lights, vibrant even over the lights of the town, they seemed especially vivid over the hospital, driving back the storm clouds. The rain lost its edge and the wind died. Thunder grumbled once more to the south and then all was quiet.

She took that as a good sign and returned to work just in time to hear that the poor youth had stopped seizing and had even woken up a little.

"Mom?" he croaked and then fell asleep.

In all the rejoicing, no one saw the lights above the town arc like massive wings and then slowly fade from sight.

The man outside the hospital shook his jacket, raindrops flying. He turned up his collar against the night air and looked south.

***

Despite everything, Evelyn must have fallen asleep since the buzzing of her phone woke her up. It was still dim outside, but there was a smear of light to the east heralding the sun. The storm had blown itself out in the night. She rolled over to grab her phone and saw that it was the hospital. Wide awake now, she grabbed it, hit the receive button, and headed for the far corner of the room.

"This is Evelyn."

"We have some good news for you," the doctor said warmly. "Your son woke up last night and asked for you. He did have a rather bad series of seizures, but he seems to have come through them."

Evelyn felt limp with relief. "Can I see him?"

"Visiting hours begin at 8," she said, her voice edged with sympathy. "We have to keep him here for another day or two to run those tests and make sure the seizures don't come back."

"Of course," Evelyn said. "Thank you for letting me know."

The phone clicked as the doctor let her go and she held it tightly against her chest. Relief made her legs feel like water and she was gasping for air. She didn't know whether to wake up Christopher and Zan and share the joy or simply hold on to the moment for a little longer.

In the end, she couldn't keep the good news to herself and woke up Christopher and Zan. Zan bounded awake as she always did, the good news buoying her even more. Christopher grumbled himself awake, but he was glad to hear that his brother was feeling better.

Dawn traced watery yellow fingers over the sky as Evelyn threw the curtains back, feeling as though she'd dropped a hundred pounds off her back.

"As soon as we can, we'll go see him," she told Christopher. "I don't know if he'll be awake, but at least he won't be in that coma anymore. He's probably exhausted."

They went to the hospital as soon as they could and were ushered into Simon's room. His eyes fluttered awake when Evelyn sat beside him, and he groaned.

Mom?" he asked, his voice cracking.

"I'm here," Evelyn said.

He grinned a little at her and then winced. His throat hurt and his arm still had the IV in it. "Where am I?"

"The hospital in Terrace," Evelyn said. "You don't remember anything?"

"I was out in the forest," he said. "I'm sorry, mom. I wanted to find Shawn's cousin." He went red with shame. "I don't know what happened though. I was looking in a clearing I found and then it started to rain, and I felt funny. I tried to go home, and everything went dark."

"You're safe now," Evelyn said. "They just want to check you over, try to figure out what happened, and make sure this doesn't happen again. Then we can go home."

He nodded. "I'm hungry."

Zan chuckled and Christopher launched himself at his brother which provoked a cry of outrage from the bedridden youth. The doctor came in a moment later and smiled at the scene.

"Seems your family is happy to have you back," she said, and Simon wrinkled his nose and tried to shove his brother off, mostly only succeeding in shoving Christopher to the side where he continued to cling like a leech.

"We're going to run the EEG and EKG today," she continued to Evelyn. "Probably a CAT And MRI too, if not today, then tomorrow. This was hopefully just a one-off incident that we can mark as 'weird but harmless', but we want to be sure. He'll have to stay for a couple of days, and we'll go over the results with you when they come in."

"Thank you," Evelyn said, and the doctor moved to Simon and began to ask him how he was feeling, checking his limbs, eyes, and head, and removing the IV. Zan put a hand on Evelyn's shoulder and smiled at her.

"I knew he'd be fine," she said, and Evelyn huffed out a snort.

"You did not."

Zan grinned at her. "I'll get everyone some breakfast. I assume they'll only get you out of here by force."

"Me?" Evelyn laughed. "Look at Christopher! They'll have to pry him off with a crowbar."

Zan laughed as well. "Don't forget to text Shawn and tell him Simon is okay."

"Right," Evelyn said. "He won't have to make the trip out today."

Zan smirked. "He might anyway." On that note, she sauntered out and Evelyn shook her head.

***

At the moment Shawn got the message about Simon, he was talking to the police at the Prince Rupert precinct.

There was little love lost between his family and the police and even less trust, but the only way Shawn could see to point the police away from suspecting Evelyn was to answer their questions. No, he hadn't seen Kal around and he hadn't even really met the guy. Evelyn had never met Lori. He couldn't think of any reason for Lori to be at Evelyn's house except that sometimes she took it in her head to wander away from the village. No, he couldn't think of anyone who would want to hurt her.

The case was clearly stumping everyone. There was no sign of injury on her, and the toxicology report came back with little more than alcohol in her system and not even enough to make her pass out, let alone kill her. The only thing he had heard were whispers that her face had been twisted up in agony, fear, and even a touch of ecstasy.

He shuddered.

They would release her back to her family later in the day. They had run all the tests they could and come up with no reason why she should be dead. All they could do now was track down Kal and interrogate him. *And they've been failing abysmally at that too.*

It was strange that no one had seen Kal. He wasn't the type of person to be very social, at least according to Evelyn, but Terrace wasn't a big town, and neither was Prince Rupert. The gardener seemed to have vanished, though, lending credence to the theory that he had killed Lori.

Though *how* bothered Shawn. Closely followed by *why*.

The text from Evelyn cheered him and he reminded himself to visit the family again and check in. He might also spot Kal in Terrace and be able to point the police in the right direction.

For now, it was time to support his family in their grief and help put his cousin to rest.

***

All Simon's test came back negative, and Evelyn frowned a little at the doctor.

"It could have been something related to lightning," the doctor said, the tests under her fingers. "He showed no sign of being struck, but if something struck nearby and the shockwave may have contributed to his collapse and seizures."

"There was no lightning at the time," Evelyn argued.

"Then for now, aside from keeping an eye on him, you'll simply have to think of this as an anomaly," the light-haired woman sighed. "I know how frustrating that is, but the human body is much more complex than we give it credit for and sometimes things go... strange."

"Strange," Evelyn repeated, shaking her head.

"I'm sorry I don't have more for you," the doctor said. "All Simon's tests show he is a normal and healthy eleven-year-old boy. Fortunately, this incident seems to have done no lasting harm."

"Can he come home then?"

"I'm getting his discharge papers done now," she said. "Keep an eye on him, and if he shows signs of anything abnormal – headaches, vision problems, dizziness, lethargy, vertigo, that sort of thing, bring him back to Prince Rupert or here."

"I will," Evelyn said. "Thank you."

Christopher was thrilled that his brother was coming home, Evelyn was thinking of her own bed after the last few nights in a hotel, and Simon seemed happy to be finally out of the hospital. They were just getting ready to leave, Zan helping to load the boys, when Evelyn saw a familiar face across the street. She waved to Zan to wait for a moment, and then dashed across the road to see Kal lounging on a patio chair outside a nail salon.

"What are you doing *here*?" she demanded. "The police are looking for you."

Kal blinked at her. "Why?"

"They want to talk to you about something they found on *my* property," she said. "You need to see them."

Kal studied her. "Something has badly frightened you."

"*You* need to see the cops," she repeated.

"All right," he said, stretching in place. Although he hadn't been to the house since the accident, the smell of flowers and earth still hung around him. "I did know that the police were there and thought it best to stay away. I see now that the decision may have been incorrect. I also heard your son was ill and taken to the hospital."

"He's better now," Evelyn said guardedly.

"I'm glad to hear it. Will you tell me why the police wish to see me?"

"I don't know if I should."

A frown knitted his brow, but he stood up in a fluid motion. "Are you now returning home?"

"Yes," Evelyn said, baffled. "Where else would I go?"

"Be careful," he said and walked away, heading, she hoped, for the police station.

Confused, but having done her civic duty, Evelyn returned to her vehicle and a puzzled Zan.

"That was Kal," she said. "The police have been looking for him, so I sent him to them."

"If he's been trying to avoid them, he's not going to go," Zan pointed out.

Evelyn pointed to the text message she just sent to Shawn:

Kal in Terrace, spotted him near the hospital. I sent him to the police, but he may not actually go.

"At least the right people will know he's in town," Evelyn said, starting up her SUV and heading out of the parking lot. "But I can't imagine him killing someone."

"We didn't do it, and if Kal didn't do it, then who did?"

Evelyn shook her head and looked through the rear-view mirror at her boys. They were looking out the windows, clearly eager to leave. "I don't know."

***

Kal stood outside the police station and considered it.

Much like the rest of Terrace, it was a low building, dusky red-brown in colour with square windows tucked under eaves. The carved figures of the totem pole stared at him, dismissive and bored. The red and black paint was faded, and the wood was gray with age. He thought about rubbing the fin of the killer whale on the bottom for luck, and then thought better of it.

Some things weren't meant to meet so flippantly.

Like him and the police.

But he told Evelyn he would check in with them, for all the good it would do them. He hadn't killed the woman, though he had been present for the aftermath and helped put her to rest when she had been tossed aside. He supposed he should have left her *in situ*, but it was disrespectful.

He glanced at Eagle sitting atop Killer Whale, but the bird had neither knowledge, nor healing, it cared to impart on him. He wouldn't touch the totem, but he bowed to it.

Respect, if not a greeting. Killer Whale coolly watched him enter the precinct.

A few hours later, it watched him come back out again. He looked tired, strangely gaunt, worn, and thin, but he was free. The police officers behind him would have to start their investigations anew. Kal was scratched off as a suspect and would shortly be completely forgotten.

"*Hat'agm haayk,*" whispered something behind him and he nodded. It was all the warning he was going to get from the totem and though he already knew what they were talking about, it was good to get confirmation that he wasn't the only one seeing it.

"Bad spirit indeed," he said aloud.

Of course, the police had left him off the hook, but Evelyn was a lot less likely to and it was her whom Kal was more concerned with. He glanced over his shoulder at the totem pole, but it simply loomed in the gathering darkness.

"A bit of wisdom wouldn't go amiss," he said, but he got the distinct feeling that this wasn't their fight anymore, if indeed it ever had been. He had to concede their point, and made his way back to the squatting house in the mountains.

Chapter Sixteen

The police had been surprisingly gentle with Evelyn's home and yard. When they returned under a purple dusk the front porch light was on, and the living room and kitchen were clean. The mound of dirt behind the greenhouse gave them all a morbid shiver, though. Zan and Evelyn threw a quick supper together, but Simon only nibbled, and Christopher was glued to his side, much to his eye-rolling annoyance.

"You're not sleeping in my room," he declared, and Christopher looked heartbroken.

"Simon needs his space too," Evelyn said, though a part of her wanted to hold on to her oldest son and never let go too. She had to console that part with frequent hair ruffles and shoulder squeezes, which Simon tolerated.

"Are you sure you even want to stay here anymore?" Zan asked once the boys were in bed. They were sitting on the back porch, trying not to look at the greenhouse. "You could just put the place up for sale as is and come back south. It might not sell as well since the… incident… but still."

"I'm not ready to go back yet," Evelyn said immediately and was shocked at her defensive tone. "I mean…"

Zan frowned. "There's something *weird* about this place, and Kal. Your son had a medical emergency out in the woods and collapsed, and the doctors still don't know why. Isn't that enough of a reason to leave?"

"It..." She felt as though her words were being caught in a tug of war between her brain and her mouth. "I'm not ready to go back to Coquitlam yet," she managed to say, though part of her was screaming quietly that she *was* ready and wanted to flee *right now.* "And the doctors may want to do more follow-up on Simon."

Zan put her elbows on her knees and glared at her best friend. "This is insane," she declared, and Evelyn cringed. "I get family loyalty and all, but what about loyalty to your kids and yourself? You said yourself you hadn't talked to your uncle in years, so why are you risking everything for this house?" She thumped the porch rail with her fist to underscore her point.

"It's *my house*," Evelyn snapped back, all fear buried under sudden rage. "Whatever is going on here, it's *mine* to deal with."

"But it *isn't*," Zan insisted. "Just sell the damn place and *move on.*"

They glared at each other, the air between them shuddering with the threat of a shattered friendship. It may well have broken at the next thing someone said, except that the next voice they heard was Kal's.

"And you!" they both said, rounding on the startled man who held up his hands in self-defence.

"What are you doing here?" Evelyn snarled, getting to her feet. "The police should have you."

"Not anymore," Kal said, backing up a pace. "I talked to them and told them what I was doing the night the woman was killed. I was nowhere near here and I had a few people able to verify that. They let me go."

Evelyn still felt as though she was thrumming with rage, but as Kal continued to look at her, she felt it breaking. "Well, that still doesn't explain what happened or why you're so... so... *weird.*"

Kal stared at her, and the rage shattered into embarrassment. Zan stood up as well, but she looked as surprised as Kal at Evelyn's outburst.

"Weird?" Kal said, mouthing the word as though it was a new food he was eating. "How do you mean?"

"I..." She suddenly felt stupid, immature, and humiliated. "I don't know. I shouldn't have said that. I'm sorry."

"It's been a rough few days," Zan said diplomatically. "I think we need some sleep."

"I just thought I'd let you know I've returned," Kal said. "I'm going to camp near the greenhouse if you don't mind. Just in case something else happens."

Evelyn then felt deeply guilty on top of stupid, with a worm of fear at her own rage. "Thank you," she mumbled. "I'm sorry."

He gave her a warm smile. "You are forgiven, of course. It's been a difficult time. Your friend is right; you should all get some sleep. I'll make sure no one sneaks in or out of the woods tonight." He wandered back towards the greenhouse with a dark bundle that proved to be a small tent.

"Open mouth, insert foot," Evelyn said.

"Bedtime," Zan answered. "Things will look better in the morning."

***

He didn't need to sleep, but to maintain the illusion, he went into his tent and settled against the wall of the greenhouse. His jacket creaked under his weight, and he frowned in annoyance as his shoulder blades began to itch and burn. He kept an eye on the house and as soon as the lights were all dark, he stepped back out of the tent and stretched. The itching and burning stopped at once.

Nothing seemed to be moving, but he kept his eyes pinned on the house anyway. His diligence was eventually rewarded: the back door opened.

The figure standing on the back porch didn't look right. It was too big to be the children, and too bulky to be Zan or Evelyn. He narrowed his eyes as the figure came down the steps and headed for the greenhouse. It clearly hadn't noticed Kal, or it didn't care.

Kal narrowed his eyes. *There's something wrong here.*

The figure was male, though it flickered strangely in the moonlight, shifting from a large figure to a smaller, female one. He had to shake his head a few times before it settled into the figure of a tall man.

"Who are you?" Kal challenged.

"Get out," the figure hissed. "You're not welcome here."

Kal crossed his arms over his chest. "I doubt very much you are either," he said. "Parasite."

The being's eyes flared bright green and Kal felt a weird pressure on his forehead and chest. It only lasted for a moment before it snapped, and he smiled. "That won't work on me. I ask again: Who are you?"

"This is *mine*," the man said, and his voice hit a weird double harmonic where Kal was sure he heard Evelyn's voice buried beneath the brass. "You have no *jurisdiction* here. No *contract*."

That gave Kal an excellent idea of what he was dealing with, but not what to do about it that wouldn't burn down the house, wreck the yard, or possibly kill someone. He wasn't about to let anything like *doubt* show on his face; ignoring the fact that the ghost would jump on it, the idea was personally foreign to him, though he saw plenty of it on those around him. Instead, he took a pace forward and rolled his shoulders.

The man met him, his hands curled into a facsimile of claws. He was larger than Kal, both in height and girth, the memory of a man who went hunting, fishing, and built much of the house behind him. Kal was smaller, his muscles atrophied from his time here, and cut off from everything he once had, but deep in him, he felt the embers of who he was rekindle.

It would have to be enough.

The larger man swung at him, and he could swear he saw claws growing to replace the fingernails. He slid aside, his breath puffing in night air that had the acrid edge of sulphur blunted by the sharp smell of sage. Far from being alarmed at that, Kal grinned.

"I see someone already locked you down," he taunted. "The divinity of the Tsy'mysen may be foreign to us, but no less powerful for it."

The spirt snarled at him and he saw the blurry contours of Evelyn underneath. If the spirt was hoping that would throw him off, he was wrong and he would discover that to his sorrow. Kal threw his shoulder into the body the spirit had built up for itself and, startled by his charge, the spirit missed a step and stumbled.

Kal straightened up suddenly and slammed his hand on his opponent's forehead, fingers splayed. "Be*gone.*"

There was a flash of gold, a furnace blast of heat, and both combatants staggered away from each other. Kal shook his fingers. They stung and he could already see welts rising from being forced to channel his essence through a body. He looked up to see Evelyn sprawled on the grass, her nightgown in disarray, her dark hair a messy halo, and her face bloodless. She was unconscious and wouldn't remember any of this come morning.

"Blood will out," he said. "And it's too late to back out now."

He sighed, picked her up, and carried her back inside and up to her room. Fortunately, the house was still quiet, no one demanding an explanation that he had no intention of giving.

***

She felt powerful in her dreams, strong and connected to the world around her in a way that she wasn't in her waking hours. She laughed off her ex-husband's pleas to return home, she kept her boys safe, and the thing in the attic was like dust and shadows, meaningless. The man behind her cheered her on, his eyes blue and savage. She strode through the house and then into the yard, feeling her ownership over it as complete as though it were merely an extension of her body. No more regrets over the divorce, nothing but disdain for her previous job, and not even a thought for what Zan or anyone else would think of her now.

But then it all went wrong. Something *slammed* into her head and suddenly she was just... Evelyn again.

Scared.

Her body returned to her, cold and weak.

Her memories slicing into her until she forced them away. An impression of feathers brushing her face and eyes staring deep into her, burning with judgement.

She wept and woke up, still crying, shaken, her heart galloping in her chest. She wasn't sure whether she was grieving or having a panic attack, but she felt awful.

Thankfully, both the boys and Zan were still asleep, and the house was quiet. She lay in bed, marshalling her thoughts and convincing her body to move. Then she slowly got out of bed and made her way downstairs to put on coffee.

The mountains were misty, and tendrils crept through the trees to brush the grass. She opened the back door, and the cool air greedily came in, rustling her bathrobe and making her ankles tingle. It was nearly August, but that seemed to mean little up in the hills. Birds chirped sleepily at each other, and at the edge of the trees, she briefly saw a deer grazing before something spooked it and sent it dashing back into the undergrowth.

It was an idyllic scene and the nightmare, or dream, faded. By the time the coffee pot was done bubbling, she had no more memories of the nightmare.

Zan came into the kitchen next, rubbing her eyes. "It stopped raining!"

"For now, at least," Evelyn said, smiling a bit at her.

"We should get out of the house and do something fun today," Zan said firmly. "No hospitals or renovations or errands."

Evelyn frowned slightly, but she forced herself to nod. "That sounds like a good idea," she said, wondering why she had felt a jolt of anger at the suggestion. "I'll get the boys up."

Zan knew that it would take several minutes for Simon to get up, so she took her coffee outside and watched the mist retreat back into the forest as the sun rose. It was beautiful outside, but something about the yard still spooked her; it felt strangely hollow. She tapped her fingers on the porch railing and watched as Kal unfolded himself from the tent he had put up against the greenhouse.

He did stay. For some reason, weird as he was, the thought gave her the first warm feeling she'd had since arriving. It almost felt like *hope*.

The gardener stretched and Zan rubbed her eyes. She must have been more tired than she thought. The shadows from the greenhouse and the way the jacket stretched conspired to make it look as though he was not just stretching his arms, but beautiful black wings as well. She rubbed her eyes hard, and the wings disappeared, leaving behind a dishevelled and sleepy looking man, entirely ordinary.

This place is getting to my head.

She knew she should go back inside, but the looming presence of the house was distasteful compared to the warm sunshine and watching Kal drag out tools for the morning's work. He was stronger than he appeared; the massive bags of dirt were slung over his shoulders like they were soft blankets, and he moved at a brisk pace. He looked a little startled when he spotted Zan, but then he smiled at her in greeting.

"Did you sleep all right?" he asked, coming her way. He put the dirt down beside the steps and rolled his shoulders.

"Yeah," Zan said. "I can't believe you stayed in a tent all night though."

Kal shrugged. He did look more tired than usual and the fingers on his right hand looked red. He must have slept on it wrong. "The bears and moose don't tend to wander here in the summer, so that wasn't a problem. The police may have released me, but I don't feel comfortable in Terrace or Prince Rupert either. Too many people will still be talking about what happened."

"Wasn't it cold?"

"I have a thermal sleeping bag."

He gazed at her a moment longer as though waiting to see if she would continue the conversation. When she didn't, he heaved the bag of dirt back on his shoulders and headed off around the house, presumably to work on some of the flowerbeds. Zan sat down on the stairs.

He still vaguely spooked her, even if he had camped out all night to keep an eye on things. And she couldn't help feeling as though he had done it for hidden reasons, though she couldn't imagine what those would be.

The house still made her feel a lot worse than he did, though. She half turned to look at it and could swear that the curtains in the attic window fluttered as though someone had been looking outside and closed them just as she looked up.

***

Evelyn thought she was feeling back to normal as she got the boys ready to go, but as they headed out to her van, she started to look a bit gray, and the boys were limp and exhausted. They weren't even picking on each other like they normally did. Zan frowned.

Normally, she likely would have sent everyone back to bed with some books or a tv show, but something was driving her to pull them out of the house and away from its influence, so she pretended she didn't see their shadowed eyes and pale faces and chattered buoyantly about the beach and ice cream instead. This at least had the effect of reviving Christopher, but Simon still looked perilously close to making a run for his room. He had his hands jammed in his pockets and looked like every sulky, rebellious teen Zan had ever known (and been herself).

"Zan is right," Evelyn said when Simon started trying to sidle back to the house. "We need to do something fun and away from here. It's finally sunny and we're going to take advantage of it."

Simon looked sullen, but he let the two women haul him out to the vehicle. They started down the driveway, but Evelyn started feeling more and more tired as they drove by the trees. The chatter of ravens nearby startled her, but it didn't do much to break through the feelings of exhaustion. Her vision blurred as she felt as though her bones were made of lead. Even moving the wheel to avoid potholes was a monumental effort.

"Evelyn," Zan said in alarm. "What's wrong?"

"I don't know," Evelyn said and even her voice sounded heavy and dull. "I'm really tired."

"I'll drive," Zan said. "Stop and let's switch."

That seemed like too much bother. She could only stare out the window and keep her foot on the gas pedal. Out of the corners of her eyes, she could see the weird bone figures, swinging, urging her on.

Now the boys sensed that something was wrong. Christopher leaned in his car seat, anxiously looking at the branches whipping the windows, and Simon chewed his lip. "Mom..." he said in a warning tone. "The trees!"

"Aunt Zan," Christopher whimpered. "What's wrong with mom? Is she drunk?"

"She's not drunk," Simon retorted.

"Evelyn," Zan said, shaking her shoulder, but it was no good. The woman seemed to be in a deep stupor and the van only went faster, between the incline and her foot heavy on the pedal. "Evelyn!"

The minivan was solid, but the road was pitted, and the branches of the trees hung over it. The sound of them slapping the sides made Zan feel like they were in a pop can being whipped down a hill. She mentally counted and realized that at this speed, they were going to shortly hit the highway and while it was *unlikely* they would meet any traffic, it wasn't impossible, and the way Evelyn looked, she might take them straight into the channel.

Decision made, Zan reached over and wrenched the steering wheel hard while slamming her foot on the brakes. Thankfully, she was taller and leggier than Evelyn and was able to work around her. Her best friend felt more like a wooden doll than a human, letting her steer them sideways and stop so hard that the wheels threw up a shower of rocks.

Christopher screamed and Simon grimly held his brother, his mind whipping back to his father totalling their car on the highway median barrier. The figure in his pocket, which he was glad no one had taken from him while he was in the hospital, was a comforting weight, holding him to his seat.

The minivan creaked and rocked, but ultimately held steady. They were staring straight into the dark forest and the sharp smell of burned rubber filled the air. A raven screamed overhead. Zan didn't realize she was gasping for breath until she heard herself. She was shaking.

Evelyn still looked like a doll, staring vacantly into the trees. Zan had kicked her foot off the gas pedal so at least they weren't in any danger of driving off into the trees, but she gave no reaction to the near collision and sudden stop.

"Are you boys okay?" Zan asked, her voice trembling.

"We're fine," Simon said. "What's wrong with mom?"

"I don't know," Zan said. She looked back at the boys to make sure for herself that they were in one piece. They were wide-eyed and Christopher had tears running down his face, but their seatbelts had held, and they were both moving without any signs of pain.

She turned back to Evelyn and froze.

Her best friend was still staring through the windshield, but when Zan tried to see what she was looking at, she was arrested by the glass itself. Reflected faintly in the glass was not Evelyn, but a *man*, grinning almost too widely for any human, his blue eyes like ice enshrouding bright candles. His features were gaunt with a pointed nose and brown hair that was swept over his forehead. She couldn't see much more of him; only his face, grinning back at Evelyn and seemingly *talking*, though Zan couldn't actually hear anything.

She screamed – she could hardly help herself – and the boys yelled. Without thinking, she scrambled out of the minivan and then ripped open the back door and helped Christopher out of his car seat, keeping her eyes firmly pinned on the buckles. Christopher let her carry him out and Simon scrambled out the other side.

"What's going on?" Simon demanded while Christopher buried his face in Zan's leg.

"I saw something," Zan said shortly. She looked at Simon and bit her lip. "Can you get Christopher back to... No..." She wanted to rip her hair out. The *house* was hardly safe, but Port Edward was too far away and there was no way she was sending the boys to walk there on their own. But if something bad was about to happen, they couldn't stay here either. Paralyzed with indecision, she tried to think through her panic.

There was no other way to do things.

"Take Christopher back to the house, but *don't go inside*," she compromised. "I have to get your mom out of there."

"I don't want to leave you," Christopher said, muffled against her jeans.

"We'll find Kal," Simon said, snapping his fingers. "Kal can help. And maybe Shawn is coming."

Zan wrung her hands. *I hate being the damsel in distress, but it would be fantastic if Shawn just happened to show up.* "Go," she said, gently pulling Christopher off her. "We're only a kilometre or so away. Stick to the middle of the road, watch out for wildlife, and go as quickly as you can. Stay outside when you get there or check the greenhouse for Kal. Hopefully your mother and I will be right behind you."

Simon nodded and took his brother's hand. Christopher burst into tears, but Simon dragged him up the road and back home. Zan scrubbed a hand over her eyes, barely noticing the large raven winging its way along the trees, seemingly keeping pace with the boys. She decided to take it as a good omen while she was left to face the minivan, which was still clicking quietly to itself from being stopped in such an obnoxious manner.

"Right," she said aloud. "It was just a faint reflection. I probably imagined it."

Unlikely, since she'd never seen anyone like *him* before, but still. She squared her shoulders and went to the driver's door. *I just won't look at the windshield.*

Evelyn was still sitting where Zan had left her, but when she started to unbuckle her friend, Evelyn's hand suddenly lashed out and grabbed Zan's wrist. She looked up at, Zan who was frozen with fear, and grinned a grin that was too wide for her face.

"How rude of you to try to leave," she whispered in a voice that was decidedly not her own. "And after all I did to make you welcome."

Zan would normally have had no problem pulling her wrist out of Evelyn's grasp, but this time it was like she was being held by iron. She yanked, but to no avail. Evelyn yanked back and Zan was slammed into the vehicle, winding her slightly and sending her to her knees. Evelyn leaned down.

"My family will *never leave*," she whispered into Zan's ear, and then she shoved her so hard that Zan fell on her butt. Evelyn laughed at her, loud and long, raucous cackles ricocheting off the uncaring trees.

"Oh, fuck off right now," Zan growled, brushing herself off and clenching her fists at her side. "No disembodied reflection of a face is telling *me* where to go."

She grabbed a large rock off the side of the road, happy that it was surprisingly sharp, and strode back to the minivan. Evelyn was still laughing, her blue eyes glittering with malice, but Zan ignored her. Instead, she went to the front of the vehicle and heaved the rock at the passenger side of the windshield as hard as she possibly could.

The laughter turned to screams of fury and cursing, but the windshield was now decorated with massive cracks. Evelyn screamed in rage and then Zan heard her suddenly go quiet.

Terrified of what she'd see, she ran back to the driver's side to see Evelyn slumped against the seatbelt, her eyes closed. There was glass on the passenger seat, but Evelyn's side was clean. Zan unbuckled her and hauled her out of the van and away from it. She was panting with both fear and anger, her arms burning from throwing the large rock.

"Fuck you, whatever the fuck you are," she panted. "No one tells me what to do."

That struck her as hilarious, and she started giggling hopelessly and couldn't stop herself until Evelyn groggily woke up in her arms.

"What's going on?" she asked in a daze.

"I wrecked the van," Zan said, wiping tears from her eyes. "Because of a man's reflection in the windshield."

"What?!"

Zan throttled the hysterical giggles still trying to well up. "We have to get back to the house," she said. "I smashed the hell out of the windshield and the boys are already going home. Can you walk?"

"The boys! Are they alright?" Evelyn struggled to her feet and swayed, but with Zan's arm around her shoulders, she found her balance.

"They're scared, but I didn't want them hanging around here. I don't know what happened and I didn't want to risk them. I sent them home to find Kal or hope that Shawn showed up." Zan shrugged weakly. "They probably haven't gotten home yet. It's only been a few minutes."

Evelyn shook her head. "We need to get to them."

"Let's go then," Zan said. "We'll deal with the minivan once we know the boys are safe. No one but Shawn and Kal come up this way anyway and Kal has a motorcycle. We can use my truck to tow your van."

"Right," Evelyn said. She staggered a few steps, but steadied and they started walking up the road. "I don't... What happened?"

"I don't know," Zan said. "I was hoping you could tell me. You went completely wooden, and we would have crashed into the highway, so I turned the van and braked it. Then..." Her voice trailed. "I don't know," she said. "Something was staring at you, and you started acting... different. I smashed the windshield, and you snapped out of it. Sorry about that."

"No," Evelyn said. "If it got me out of... whatever... Then it was worth it. I can repair the windshield."

"We'll tow it to Prince Rupert," Zan said. "Surely there's a repair shop there. I'll pay for it."

"Uncle Jason is paying for it," Evelyn said firmly. "Don't worry about it."

They sped up their pace and soon caught up with the boys. Christopher launched himself at his mother, still crying, and even Simon stayed close to her. They made their way back to the house, shaken and confused, feeling as though the old house was no sanctuary at all.

Chapter Seventeen

Once the ceremonies and the funeral were over, such as Covid allowed, there should have been a feeling of closure, but Shawn felt the opposite. The police were baffled, there were no leads, and no reason why Lori should have been at Evelyn's house, let alone how she died there and ended up in a shallow grave. Aside from his aunts and father, though, Shawn felt as though very few people were grieving or demanding answers in a meaningful fashion.

It could be argued that the people of Port Edward and even Prince Rupert and Terrace had become so accustomed to grieving their women that it barely registered anymore. It simply added to the weariness, the disdain for the police, and the malaise that came from neglect. His aunt received plenty of condolences, as did the rest of the family, but then everyone returned to their bubbles.

Lori was turned to a statistic. Another Northwest coast death, another corpse to add to the pile that addiction and intergenerational trauma had built. It was the same pile Shawn's mother had been dumped on when she took her own life five years past.

But while Lori had certainly been a child of trauma and certainly had her demons, he couldn't believe she had taken

Inheritance

her own life or had been killed by the same murderers haunting the Highway of Tears. He combed through her last Facebook and Instagram posts, trying to figure out if there were clues in her posts. He watched her last TikTok videos (mostly her slurring her way through talking trash about her ex), looking for any clues as to what could have killed her.

He always circled back to her last Facebook post. Who promised her she would forget? And forget what?

He poured over her digital life until his eyes blurred and forced him to drop into a restless slumber, where he chased the phantom figure of his cousin until she disappeared in a wash of red fog.

Then a woman stood in front of him and for a moment he didn't recognize her. She was shorter than him, with long gray hair swept up in tight braids. Her regalia was bright red and black, proudly bearing the Raven. She had her arms crossed when he saw her, but she reached out for him a moment later.

"'*Niit łukda'aynm 'yuuta,*" she said.

"Hello, grandmother," Shawn said, startled. "What are you doing in my dreams?"

She smiled at him. "Where else would I talk to you, silly child?" she said affectionately. "I can't exactly visit you for tea."

"I suppose not," he said ruefully. "But why are you here to talk to me?"

She gestured behind her, and he looked, but only dimly saw what looked to be a couple of totem poles looming in the fog.

"The colonizers may have sworn off bringing old brands of evil, but that doesn't stop the individuals from doing so," she said. "I was warned and told to warn you. It took your cousin, and it is taking your friend Evelyn. The divine being who guards her home has had his wings clipped. He cannot defeat it alone, nor can she, nor can you."

She clapped her hands together, once. We tried, my daughters and I, and you see the results. One no longer rests easy and lost many of her memories, I died, and one now drinks herself into a stupor, having lost her daughter." She quirked a malicious smile. "But we dulled its claws."

Shawn frowned. "If *you* couldn't cleanse the house, grandmother..."

"It walks the border between the Tsy'mysen and the white people," she said. "Taking protection and sustenance from both."

"I've never heard of anything like that," Shawn said.

"No, this creature is entirely new. The one who became this spirit broke the boundaries between the spirit worlds. He is made from death and blood and fouled land."

Shawn clenched his fists. "This thing was *alive?*"

"You know who it was," his grandmother said. "We didn't see the danger then. But now it's too late to reclaim the man, and the land demands a purge it cannot undertake alone. I am sorry, *łukda'aynm 'yuuta*. Your father cannot help you, nor can your aunts. I wouldn't ask that of them again."

Shawn heaved a sigh. "What can I do?"

Inheritance

She held up a few fingers and for a weird moment, he felt like he was standing in her kitchen again, learning how to can salmon.

"Burning sage harmed it, drove it into the underground and attic. But now it feeds on the fear of Evelyn and her children. It trapped your cousin in the mirrors where it lives, and slowly corrupts her to its purpose. They must face their bloodline without that fear and starve it. This will give their guardian the chance to act. Burn sage in the attic and basement, drive it out, give it no place to hide." She frowned. "You must learn *why* it has attached itself to Evelyn and her children. No mere uncle she barely knew could have done this to her."

"He lied about being her uncle?"

"Perhaps," she said. "Or else found something that bound itself more strongly to her. Perhaps there is something to be found in the house."

"She's not going to believe me," Shawn sighed.

"She will either be forced to believe or have herself or her boys taken as a vessel." His grandmother sighed. "I would hope she is more than an empty cup."

Me too, Shawn thought grimly. "Thank you, *Nts'Tits*."

"Be careful," she said. "I don't know how much more we are allowed to help."

He nodded and she cupped a hand around his face. "I am very proud of you, Shawn," she breathed and then faded away, leaving the smudged figures of the totem poles standing on a foggy beach. He squinted to see them better, but only saw the eyes of the Raven staring at him. They were huge and golden, with flickering flames in the middle. The Raven seemed to laugh and then swooped down and swallowed him whole.

He woke up in his own bed and stared up at the ceiling where the morning sun stretched out its fingers.

***

In contrast to Shawn, Evelyn spent the entire night wide awake, her sheets gripped in her fists. Every time she even thought about trying to go to sleep, her eyes would pop back open and she would feel terror slide its fingers up and down her spine to pool in her stomach. The alarm clock ticked the minutes by in agonizing notes.

She gave up the whole thing at two in the morning and went outside. It was dark, but the moon cast a soft glow over everything, enough to see a little by. The mountains and trees were black blotches and the house loomed over her. Zan and the boys were sound asleep after their ordeal.

She still couldn't remember any of it. She remembered getting into the minivan and then a blank spot until she woke up in Zan's arms. And no matter how hard she tried, she just couldn't bring any memories of the drive, though Christopher and Simon had filled in the blanks between sobs.

A small circle of light popped up by the greenhouse and resolved itself to be Kal. She assumed he was going into the trees to relieve himself, but he simply crawled out of the tent and stood beside it.

He must have also been feeling a bout of insomnia.

Before she could stop herself, she called out and he looked over, his flashlight bobbing over the grass. He tentatively waved and she waved back, gesturing for him to come to the back porch. She wasn't quite sure *why* she summoned him over, but she suddenly didn't want to be alone in the darkness. The light danced and hopped as he made his way over until it came to rest around her knees so she wouldn't be blinded by it.

"I know I don't sleep much," he said. "But why are you awake? I heard you had a rough morning."

She shrugged. "The boys and Zan had it worse than me," she said. "I don't even remember what happened."

He leaned against the stair railing and looked up at the stars. "Nothing to block my view," he said, but he sounded sad. "I imagine this is all still strange to you."

"I could get used to it," she said. "But I feel like coming here may have been the worse choice I've ever made, and I don't know what to do about it now. And really, does it matter?"

By the light from the flashlight, she could see his hazel eyes flickering with gold. "Oh?"

"I did everything right before. Got married, had two kids, worked hard. Married *well* for that matter. Bought the house. But then..."

"Then it all fell," Kal said.

"I think becoming an adult means learning that bad things happen to good people and it doesn't matter what you did right," Evelyn said bitterly. "My father-in-law died in the most random way possible: hit by a car. He broke his neck and died instantly. My... ex... was never the same. Laid off from his job a month later and started drinking."

"That was his choice," Kal said.

"I know," Evelyn said. "But his dad didn't choose to die. His employer laid him off just to save some money on the bottom line. My ex worked hard, you know? Loved his job, thought his boss and his team had his back. That sort of betrayal – death, job loss..."

"Do you forgive him his drinking?"

"*No*," Evelyn said vehemently. "No, he drove drunk and hurt the boys. Totalled the car, put Simon in the hospital, and Christopher had nightmares for a week after and even *that* wasn't enough to pry the bottle out. But what can I do when someone else's choices ruin my life?" She moodily kicked at the deck. "I don't even know why my uncle left me this pile."

Kal shrugged and turned his attention back to the stars. "You could have simply sold this place and not come here at all."

"This is giving me a respite before I have to find a new place to live. And a new job. It wasn't enough that my ex got fired; I got laid off as well. Gotta save that bottom line."

"Still, you had the choice. Not a good one perhaps, but a choice. Everything was a choice."

Evelyn snorted. "Next you're going to tell me that everything happens for a reason."

Kal grinned at her. "No. Everything happens here because of *choices*. Bad ones, good ones, mostly neutral ones. Thoughtful, thoughtless, well-reasoned, rash; choices. People making choices." He ran a hand over the railing. "They underestimate that power."

Not we? It was an odd way to put it, but she had the growing feeling he really did consider everyone else to be a 'they', not a 'we'.

"No one can force you to be anything but what you will yourself to be," he continued, and his tone was still thoughtful, but there was a layer of something strange. If Evelyn didn't think too hard about it, she would have said envy, but she couldn't think why that would be. "Free will is a gift. A curse, some would say, but at the end of all things, it's the greatest gift you have."

"It doesn't feel like it," Evelyn grumbled. "Being free to choose means being free to screw it all up."

He laughed a little. "I suppose. But don't forget that you can *keep* choosing, even after screwing it all up." He yawned and stretched, forcing her to shield her eyes as the light danced across her. "You may wish to choose sleep," he added. "Another day comes."

"I'm sorry for keeping you," she said, suddenly embarrassed, but he waved her off and made his way back to the tent, the white light from the flashlight moving over the grass.

Evelyn gave the house behind her a final slow look, but she clenched her fists. *Free to choose? I didn't get to choose anything that has happened to me lately.*

But, said another voice that sounded suspiciously like Zan's. *You can choose how you react to it and what you do about it.*

She supposed that right now, she should take Kal's advice. No matter what else happened, morning was still going to come. She went back inside, but didn't doze off until dawn trembled at the edge of the sky.

A huge raven pecked at seeds that had been dropped accidentally around the greenhouse, and then spat them out in disdain. He ruffled his feathers.

"You won't find much more food for your eternally empty stomach here, Txaamsm," Kal murmured from the door of the tent. "Respect and apologies."

The raven tilted his head. *"White man's God spirit,"* he rasped deep in his throat. Kal grinned.

"I do have some of The People's fish, if you like," he said and put out the last scraps of some canned salmon he'd purchased in Terrace. The raven sighed, but hopped over and ate it.

"You speak with respect for a representative of the New God," the raven decided. *"But your wings are clipped."* He tilted his head. *"You asked too many questions."*

"Always," Kal said dryly. "And now I'm here to clean up a mess."

The raven seemed to laugh. *"I sent one of The People to help, if he's not too thick-headed to realize it. My daughter and daughter's daughters tried and clipped the demon's talons. It has stewed over that these past months."*

Kal looked at the house. "He is rooted deep."

"Like a poisoned cedar. And the poison spreads."

"I hope I did a little good before," Kal said, taking down his tent while the raven stalked around his feet. "Only time will tell."

"Mortals don't have enough time to wait," the raven warned and flew up to the roof of the greenhouse. *"Thank you for the fish,"* he added. *"May your wings return to you one day."*

Kal shrugged. "That is up to my Creator," he said, and the raven laughed and took to the wing.

"I *do not clip the wings of those who ask questions,"* Kal heard him say as he headed west towards the ocean.

"No," Kal murmured. "But your demesne is not mine. And as we can see, blurring our borders leads to greater evils."

The raven of course did not answer, but Kal wouldn't have expected him to.

Chapter Eighteen

Evelyn thought that her sanity might shatter over the two days that followed the accident on the road. They towed her SUV to Prince Rupert where they were told it would be a week or so in order to replace the windshield. They loaded up Zan's truck with groceries and more supplies for the house renovations. Evelyn thought that perhaps, if she threw herself fully into the work to fix the house up and focus on getting it ready to sell, she would be too exhausted to worry about her disrupted sleep or the horrible things that had happened.

It worked a little. Even the boys started helping, sensing perhaps that there was a light at the end of the tunnel. Simon stopped talking about wanting to stay.

The bedrooms and kitchen were painted and cleaned, the living room was repainted, and the glass in the windows was scrubbed until they sparkled. The bathroom sinks were fixed and Zan spent one memorable morning laying down new carpet in the foyer and replacing loose pieces of stair banister. Even Kal seemed to have thrown himself into making the house more appealing to others – in the August sunshine, the flowers bloomed.

Even though they worked themselves into a stupor, Evelyn still couldn't sleep properly at night. Every time she nearly dropped off, she felt as though someone was standing over her, trying to paralyze her body and whisper in her ear, jolting her awake. The shadows in the bedrooms looked like long fingers and even when she was awake, she still felt like there was a man murmuring in her ear.

And even though the house was almost finished, she still hadn't talked to anyone about putting it up for sale.

August continued its stately march towards September and one morning, they realized that they only had two areas left of the house to deal with: the attic and the basement.

"We can't just ignore them," Zan said over breakfast, but her eyes kept flicking to the basement stairs. "The basement still has junk in it, and I've never even seen the attic."

Simon and Christopher were extremely unhappy with the agenda for the day. Simon picked at his food and Christopher kept clinging to his mom's arm.

"It's scary," he said. "Last time we tried to go down there, the monster tried to get us."

Normally Zan would have laughed this off, but not this time.

"We'll be careful," she said. "If there's a monster down there, we can't sell the house to some unsuspecting schmuck." She glanced at Evelyn. "At some point *that* has to be dealt with too."

For a moment, Evelyn felt a deep, possessive rage well up in her and something of that must have made its way to her face, causing Zan to pull back a little. But she shook herself.

"Of course," she said. "I know it does. Shawn gave me a card for one of his friends who works in real estate. I'll give her a call."

"Good," Zan said. "We'll load up the truck with junk today and haul it, and then tackle the attic."

They lingered over breakfast, unwilling to leave the sunny kitchen for the gloom of the basement, but Zan finally shooed them all towards the stairs. The boys crowded on the landing, looking down, while Evelyn and Zan led the way.

"I don't think we're going to convince them to come downstairs," Evelyn said, looking back at her boys.

Zan shrugged. The basement was a lot colder than the upstairs and the darkness seemed to loom out from the corners. The stairs creaked underfoot, and she kept glancing at the gaps between them to make sure nothing was watching their descent.

The door to the butcher room was firmly closed and the boxes and equipment piled up in the main room yawned weird shadows. The only window was grimed over with old dirt and weeds, letting in only a small amount of yellow-gray light that seemed too afraid to come close.

"Maybe it's just as well they don't want to come downstairs," Evelyn continued.

By unspoken agreement, they avoided the butcher room and instead started on the main room. Once the light was on, the room was more comfortable. The yellow-white glow flooded the room and it suddenly all seemed very ordinary:

boxes, broken furniture, a few old rifles, and a beautiful set of knives that gave them both shivers. The sheet was still thrown over the mirror and there was no sign of movement.

Some of the boxes were quite heavy and when they were opened, revealed neatly stacked piles of books.

"Maybe we should sort this a bit better," Evelyn said. "These books could go to a thrift store."

Zan glanced through some of them. Most of them were fairly innocuous: old classics, old Reader's Digest hardcover collections, books on hunting, and books on plants. A few were more esoteric with titles hinting at rituals, mythology, and extremely niche histories. She shrugged. "Maybe?"

One of the boxes had a slimmer box on top of the stacked spines and when Evelyn opened it, she saw a leather book inside, unmarked. She opened it to see that it was a diary. A strange coppery smell emanated from the pages, mixed with the smell of dry paper.

"Your uncle's?" Zan asked, looking over at it.

"I guess so," Evelyn said. "This probably shouldn't go to a thrift store." She looked at the first page and was surprised to see that it was dated for thirty-three years in the past.

"Today, my daughter was born."

Zan looked up. "I didn't know you had a cousin."

Evelyn felt sick. "I don't," she said and pointed to the date: December 31, 1990. Zan looked at it, and then slowly looked back at her.

"That's your birthday," she whispered.

***

December 31, 1990

Today, my daughter was born.

I received the phone call, but there won't be any pictures because of where I'm deployed. I know that Marie is very unhappy about the timing, but we go where we must and being sent to support our allies in Kuwait is important. For now, I haven't seen much combat, but there are rumors of a massive aerial and naval invasion in the coming weeks.

We have named her Evelyn after Marie's grandmother. I'm sorry I won't be able to see you my sweet girls until my time here is over. Hopefully that is sooner than later.

January 18, 1991

I'm writing this between bombardments. It's easy to feel removed from the horrors. All I ever see are beautiful flowers of fire lighting up the ground and plumes of smoke to guide my way.

Someday, sweet Evelyn, I hope you'll understand better than your mother why I do this.

February 20, 1991

So much fire and death over oil.

I should be grieving I guess, but I actually feel released every time I shoot down another enemy. How many people can honestly say that they love what they do?

I think I'll miss this when we are done. Which probably won't be long now.

February 28

A couple of the guys flew planes to chase off the last of the Iraqis. I'm annoyed that they didn't send me, but we all have to follow the chain of command. Still, to be involved in that final rout and make sure that those Haji bastards know they were licked.

I'm not looking forward to going home. My place is here, raining death and destruction.

April 20

I returned home, but everything seems gray and dull. All I can think to do is drink beer and watch tv. Evelyn makes me smile and she's moving around more. My wife is furious and tells me I need to go into counselling.

Fuck that. I need to get back into the sky. I need to see the fire flowers and know that I hold death in my hand and can cast it out in a glittering net.

***

"I thought your father was *dead*," Zan said. Evelyn raised an eyebrow. "I meant *years* dead," she amended.

"Mom never talked about him," Evelyn said, tracing her fingers over the cover of the diary. "I asked a lot when I was a kid, but she'd basically pretend to go deaf. I learned to stop asking."

"He was in the air force. During the Gulf War."

"I guess so," Evelyn said. "Like I said, mom refused to talk about him."

Zan gave her a sideways look. "I guess leaving this house to you makes more sense now."

"He started writing me letters when I was eight or so," Evelyn said. "He introduced himself as my uncle Jason. Mom just assumed he was someone on dad's side and let it me. She was mad when he came to meet me though and I never knew why. She must have recognized him, but still didn't tell *me*."

"I wonder why?" Zan said. "You were an adult when he came up to meet Simon, so why not say anything?"

Evelyn snorted gently. "You've met my mother. She never could stand anything that took her out of the spotlight, and she loved keeping secrets. Why do I think I rarely talk to her anymore? She must have been loving the fact that she was living in a soap opera."

Zan narrowed her eyes in thought, but she didn't say anything as Evelyn tucked the diary behind her to keep it from being loaded with everything else.

It took a few runs to empty the basement room and when they were done, all that remained was the mirror which neither of them felt up to dealing with. By dinner, the room had been cleaned and light could come through the window uninhibited. Boxes of books were stacked on one wall to be donated and the mirror would be loaded with Shawn's help. The boys had been convinced to at least help put things in the truck, but they still refused to go into the basement.

"The man with the big wings told us not to," Christopher said stubbornly.

"There really wasn't anything *in* the butcher room," Evelyn said, gazing at the closed door. "We can just leave it."

"Then that just leaves the attic," Zan said.

"Not tonight," Evelyn swiftly countered.

Zan agreed and after eating supper, they drifted apart, each to their own rooms. Evelyn held her father's diary in her lap, gazing out across the trees.

The fact that the man she thought was an uncle was actually her father still had to finish making its way through the maelstrom in her head. She was furious at her mother all over again for keeping it from her, and couldn't figure out why he didn't tell her himself. And now she felt even more reluctant to sell the house, given that it really was hers by rights and the only thing she had left of the father she never really knew.

What made you leave us? It must have been very early in my life since I don't remember you.

Perhaps the diary held answers.

***

May 28, 1991

Evelyn is almost six months old. She is crawling and even trying to sit up, though her head is still too big. She has outgrown her smallest clothing and she eats more. Marie is starting to get more sleep which means she's less bitchy, but more distant.

Maybe she senses my distance.

I have been feeling a... longing... to travel again. My time with the Air Force is done, thanks to getting shot in the leg. I have something of a pension, but it's not enough to live on. Marie will be going back to work soon. I'm on disability. It's nowhere near what the government owes me, but they're never going to pay out.

Marie doesn't know about it, but my dad left me a house in the northwest. He died last month. Apparently, the house is a complete wreck, but the land may still be good.

I don't know if I even want to tell her or if I just want to leave.

I think Evelyn would grow up better without me here, drinking and swearing and complaining. Full of hate.

June 30, 1991

The northwest coast is beautiful, and I finally feel at home. The house my dad left is a complete ruin, so I'm tearing it down and rebuilding a house on the land. I hope someday Evelyn will see it.

My wife found out about it and thought we should all go. Perhaps the change of scenery would help us all. But I gave her divorce papers instead. She threw a mug at my head. I deserved it, but she deserved the bloody nose and broken arm I gave her more.

I shouldn't have done that.

But it felt good.

July 3, 1991

The ruined house was torn down today, and everything is being hauled away. I went to Port Edward and met some of the people there. They were quite friendly, especially when I mentioned I enjoyed hunting and wanted to learn more from them. Prince Rupert is small as well, but the smell of the sea is refreshing.

I've been meeting with a local business out of Terrace to get a new house built and I'm very excited. It's going to have four bedrooms so I can have guests, and after talking to the people in Port Edward, I decided to put in a butcher room as well so everyone can come after a hunt and process their kills. A few of the elders mentioned that they hunt as a community, but sometimes the weather makes it more difficult. While I don't know how much use the room will, be, I think it will be helpful to some.

Marie refuses to answer my calls and won't send me pictures of my daughter. I suppose I deserve that.

But if you ever read this, Evelyn, know that I'm also building this house for you. Someday, you'll discover the beauty of this place, like your father and grandfather did.

Several pages after that were blank and Evelyn gave them a puzzled frown. They had faint brown stains on them that she thought might have been coffee rings, but the colour looked off somehow.

The next entry was dated fifteen years later and only read:

I found the true gift from my father.

Ringing it were drawings of stick figures and bird skulls with the last few pages covered in a brown stain. When she looked more carefully, she saw that there were imprints of letters and numbers, none of which she could piece together into something that made sense. Frowning, she closed the diary again and looked around to see that it was completely dark outside. The clouds must have rolled in, covering the moon.

Dad, she thought, trying it out, but it just didn't connect with the man she sporadically spoke with on the phone and saw precisely once. She could barely think of him as an uncle, let alone her *father*.

She could have called her mom and told her off about it, but to what purpose? She had been absolutely correct in what she had told Zan, and she wasn't going to hold any illusions that her mother would break down and admit to keeping everything hidden. And it wasn't as though her mother had *lied* to her precisely; she had just refused to talk about it other than to say he was gone. And given he had broken her arm, Evelyn could hardly blame her for not wanting to talk about him.

Rain spat from the sky and slowly steadied into a downpour as she sat on her bed, wondering about her father.

Chapter Nineteen

She dreamed that the house was put up for sale, but when each of the potential buyers came to see it, she drove them off with the knives she found in the basement. This was her home now.

This was his *home. He would never let anything take it from him. She contemplated burning the For Sale sign and locked the door behind her to wrap herself in perfect quiet.*

Save for the whispers from the attic. They hungered *and promised eternal safety and power in return for being fed.*

Simon was staring up at the attic, murmuring, holding a yellow stick figure in his hand.

***

The morning was enveloped in a deep fog and Shawn had to slow his jeep to a crawl as he made his way up to the old house. In Prince Rupert, the sun had quickly burned the mist away, but here in the foothills, it hung weirdly greasy and oppressive. The silence closed around Shawn and he cranked up the radio to compensate.

There was a sudden *thud* on the top of his jeep, and he braked hard. The music stuttered to a halt, leaving the click of an annoyed engine.

Something was pecking the roof.

"I've seen this movie before," Shawn muttered, but the idea of simply listening to something unseen on his roof held the very real danger of driving him insane. He took a deep breath and then flung himself out of the jeep and away, nearly landing in the ditch.

The large raven cocked his head at him and quorked derisively. It fluttered its wings.

"Hilarious," he said crossly, standing up and dusting himself off. "Get off my jeep."

The raven hopped an insolent inch away and stared at him, daring him to do something. He was tempted to throw a fallen branch at it, but he took a deep breath instead.

Remember your dreams.

"Honoured Raven," he said. "Would you please get off my jeep?"

The raven spread his wings, jumped off, and landed on the branch of the tree beside him. He preened his feathers.

"Thanks, I guess," Shawn sighed and opened his door. There was a blur of wings and he scrambled back again as the raven flew by him, through the door, and landed on the passenger seat.

"You can *fly*," Shawn scoffed. "You don't need a *ride*."

The raven stared at him with a shiny eye, and he growled under his breath and got in the driver's seat. "I hope you're not a backseat driver," he said. "I don't need to get hit in the head with a wing."

The raven looked smug, and they carefully started their way up the road again. Shawn glanced over at his passenger; the bird was standing almost preternaturally still, only its glittering eyes and the slight fluttering of his wings to keep his balance when he bumped over potholes showed that the bird was actually alive.

The fog grew even thicker as they got higher up in the hills and soon Shawn could only see a foot or two in front of him. He could only hope that no wildlife jumped out in front of his vehicle. It was weirdly dark too; the sun was almost completely blocked by the mist and the trees crowded over him. The raven shifted from foot to foot and cocked his head as he looked intently out the window.

"We should be almost there," Shawn said uncertainly. It was hard to tell where they were, and it even felt as though they were barely moving. He knew he was going slowly, but the house wasn't *that* far up the road.

The raven suddenly flared his wings and Shawn braked again. Silence descended upon them and he could see even less than before.

"I hope you had a good reason for that," he said, but he couldn't seem to bring his voice above a whisper. The raven tapped the passenger side door and Shawn leaned over and opened it. The bird immediately took to the wing, leaving him behind.

"That can't be a good sign," he muttered, but he slammed the door shut and started the jeep again. *I have to be almost there.*

He couldn't even see where he was going anymore, but he knew it was a straight line, so he gripped the steering wheel and set forth again, trying to feel the road through the tires. The tree branches smacked his windows, but that was nothing new, and he grimly pressed on.

His jeep hit a pothole, but unlike other times where it would just continue on, it came to a grinding halt and no matter what he did to try to get it moving, the jeep stubbornly refused. The tires squealed and ground against the packed gravel, but the front end seemed to be stuck and all he was doing was digging himself in deeper.

"What the *hell?*" he cursed and thudded the steering wheel with his fists. He couldn't keep driving; he would just trash his tires. He got out instead and shook his head.

He had managed to get the jeep stuck in the perfect Death Pothole – wide enough to get him stuck, shallow enough to fool someone into thinking they could make it through. *But I shouldn't be completely stuck.*

There was a loud *caw* above him and he flung himself away from the jeep just as something crashed into it from the other side, sending it spinning around in the pothole and leaving him face to face with a Kermode bear.

The white bear and the human stared at each other. Shawn was close enough to see the flecks of gold in the bear's brown eyes and smell carrion on its breath. The bear was about three feet tall at the shoulder and its pure white fur seemed to melt and blur into the fog. It curled its mouth back, revealing yellow teeth and long claws flexed in the mud.

"Shit," Shawn said succinctly.

Running was out of the question. Even if he could see where he was going, the bear would be on him before he could go two feet. He wasn't even sure he could get in the jeep before the bear attacked him.

"Hey, bear," he said quietly, holding out his hands. "Sorry about that, didn't mean to startle you." He slowly backed towards the jeep, hoping to at least put it between himself and the animal.

The bear whuffed thoughtfully and sat on its haunches.

"Respect to you," Shawn said gently. "I'm going to help my friend who lives in the house at the end of the road. I didn't mean to intrude."

The bear watched him as he made his way to the other side of the jeep and then they regarded each other through the windows. Even with the jeep between them, Shawn felt like the bear was too close, and he kept imagining he could feel its breath on his cheek. If he made too much noise, it might go *through* his jeep.

In the fog, the bear seemed to waver strangely, its creamy fur shifting and blending with the mist. Only its eyes remained steady, locked on Shawn. He tried not to think of himself as food and must have succeeded since the bear was losing interest in him, though it also didn't seem to want to move out of the road.

Shawn wasn't sure how long they stood there, but then for no reason he could see, the bear finally stood up and ambled away, heading in the opposite direction of the house. He had the feeling that the bear going *towards* the main road wasn't exactly a good omen, but he was too relieved to see it leaving to pay it much mind.

The bear hadn't exactly helped matters with the jeep in the pothole – now it was just facing the wrong way and was still stuck. He glared at it for a moment and then looked up the road where, in the fading mist, he saw the lights of the house beckoning him forward.

Evelyn was bound to have a phone he could borrow. Sighing, he made his way the last hundred metres or so on foot.

Although it was morning, the house seemed oddly quiet – only the vehicles out front showed that anyone was there. The house loomed in the fog and the porch light, usually a hot yellow, was softly diffused. The windows were dark, and he couldn't even make out the shapes of the furniture inside.

It's not that early, he fretted. *Shouldn't they be up?*

***

The first clue that Zan had that something was wrong came when she woke up to the feeling of ropes tying her limbs. For a split second, it took her back to her college days and she almost said, "Andy?" But then she remembered that she was about fifteen years beyond her college days, and Andy had been hit by a car and killed two months after the Rope Incident.

Bleary still, she opened her eyes and then shrieked around a gag stuffed in her mouth.

She was hanging, her toes barely touching the floor, in the butcher room. Her mind blanked in panic and when she came back around, it was to Evelyn standing in front of her.

But this wasn't *her* Evelyn. Her dark, wavy hair was in knots and tangles, half over her face. Her skin was pale, almost sickly, and covered in a sheen of sweat. And her normally gray eyes were so bloodshot that the pupils looked to be in pits of fire. Zan chanced a quick look around and was relieved to see that the boys were nowhere in sight.

Now there was the issue of Evelyn standing in front of her, loosely holding a butcher knife, and the gag in her mouth that rather prevented communication beyond muffled grunts. She somehow doubted that grunting as going to shake Evelyn out of whatever was wrong with her.

But the sounds of the basement door opening at least gave Evelyn pause, enough that Zan was able to move back a little. Evelyn looked over her shoulder and then whipped back and almost quicker than Zan could see, the knife was at her throat.

I'm dead, was her last thought, and then, weirdly, the memory of Kal flashed through her mind, digging in the flowerbeds, his black coat whipping strangely in the wind. He looked up and gazed thoughtfully at her.

"*Be not afraid,*" he said, which struck Zan as a strange thing for her memory to throw up, especially given the situation.

There was a boom which sounded like thunder, the door to the butcher room slammed open, and Evelyn collapsed in a heap at Zan's feet. Zan stared down at her in shock, only a trickle of blood trailing down her neck. She looked towards the open door and saw Shawn in the doorway. He stared in shock at the scene before him.

"Mmmff," Zan said, trying to sound urgent without sounding panicked. He got the message and quickly stepped over Evelyn to cut Zan down with the butcher knife.

"What the *hell,*" Shawn said. "Where are the boys?"

"Presumably still in their rooms," Zan said, rubbing life back into her hands and hissing with pain from the scratch on her neck. "I hope, anyway."

"You check. I'll restrain... her...?"

Zan nodded and barrelled up the stairs, just as happy to leave Shawn with the collapsed form of who was once her best friend and now, she wasn't sure who it was. Thankfully, the boys were still asleep in their beds and there was no sign of anything odd or dangerous.

Downstairs, Shawn was faced with the problem of an unconscious Evelyn and nothing to restrain her with. He settled on half carrying, half dragging her back to the main floor and putting her in the bathroom, reasoning that they would be able to see her when she came out and they could decide what to do from there.

Zan was in the kitchen by the time he had settled Evelyn in the bathtub, surrounded by bottles of shampoo, conditioner, and soap so they could have a bit of rudimentary alarm system. She looked badly shaken; her mug trembled in her hand and her eyes kept flicking to the basement door.

"What happened? Shawn asked, sitting down across from her.

"I don't know," Zan said. "I was asleep, and I woke up down there with Evelyn ready to slit my throat. She didn't look... right."

"I should think not," Shawn snorted. "But why?"

Zan shook her head. "It was like she was sleepwalking, but her eyes weren't open. I don't know."

The voices were angry. Not enough blood, not enough blood, they screamed.

But just as Evelyn was sure she was going to be overwhelmed and lost forever, she was bathed in golden light and from the shadows came a man with a huge raven on his shoulder. The raven gave her an amused look while the man flared out black wings.

"Begone," he intoned, and the voices jabbered into a furious silence. The raven took to the air and landed on her stomach, staring down at her.

"We can't help you alone," the raven croaked. "You are one of the colonial god's and you do not follow his footsteps either. But then, neither does your guardian. So, we are all well matched and perhaps all together can drive him away."

"This time," the man repeated, sounding sad. "Only this time. Continue your work and drive him out for good."

"But he's my dad," Evelyn protested. She felt lonely without the voices. One of them was her father, she was sure of it.

"It's choices which shape what we are," the man said. "Are you a monster or human? Your father's shell or your own person?"

The voices had promised she would see her dad again.

But the voices probably lied. And in flashes of memory, she saw Zan dangling in front of her like a piece of meat. She clapped her hands over her eyes.

The black wings reached to the sky, filled with rainbow eyes, staring, reaching into her. She screamed and buried her face away, whimpering.

"Your friend was saved by one of mine," the raven said, his beak close to her ear. "He's here now to help you drive out the spectres of your father and your grandfather, and all their victims. But only if you go!"

The smack of feathers against her face woke her up and Evelyn found herself staring at the shower head in her bathroom. She had been weeping.

Chapter Twenty

The noise from the bathroom dragged Zan to the door, but when she tentatively looked inside, it was to see Evelyn curled up in the bathtub, her eyes looking normal again. She mostly looked confused and then when Zan explained what she was doing there, horrified.

"I don't remember anything after I fell asleep last night," she said. "Oh, Zan..."

"Shut up," Zan said good-naturedly, managing to keep the fear out of her voice. She was rather proud of that. "You weren't... *you.*"

Shawn grimaced as he helped her out of the tub.

"Are the boys okay?" she asked.

"They're fine," Zan reassured her. "Still asleep."

"I don't think you would have hurt them," Shawn said. "Zan's the one who isn't related to you and is the threat. And, well I guess I would have been as well, but I wasn't here."

Although judging from the situation he'd come in on, he *would* have been here if it hadn't been for the spirit bear and he either would have been hanging up with Zan or more likely, given that he would have been awake, dead. He shuddered.

Evelyn hugged herself. "I had a horrible dream," she said, looking distant. "But then there was a man... Or something... And a raven. A huge one."

Shawn exchanged looks with Zan, and they both shrugged. "There's a lot of weird shit happening," he said. "Kitchen. I need coffee."

"I second that," Zan said, putting an arm around Evelyn's shoulder, though she wasn't surprised when it was shrugged off. "And maybe some toast before the boys wake up and we have to act like everything is fine."

It seemed unlikely that any of them would be able to pull that off, but no one was going to point it out. And a cup of coffee steadied them.

"What are you doing here, anyway?" Zan asked Shawn.

"Good thing I was here," he retorted and then looked ashamed. "Sorry."

"No, I'm sorry," Zan said. "That was rude."

"I was driving up to check in and my sister said that someone had called her about the house. But my jeep got stuck in a massive pothole on the road, so I had to walk. I was hoping to use your phone to get a tow."

"A pothole?"

"Must have opened up in all the rain," Shawn said. "It's not like that road is well maintained."

"You can use my phone," Evelyn said. "But I didn't call your sister about the place."

Shawn looked at Zan who shrugged and shook her head.

"Well, *someone* called her about selling the place," he said. "I was just coming to see if you wanted to set a date for an open house and take a few pictures. She won't be able to come up for a few days."

"No one called," Evelyn said harshly, and Shawn raised his eyebrows. "I haven't even decided if I'm selling or not yet."

Zan gave her a long, thoughtful look. "Then why are we cleaning the place so thoroughly? I thought that was the point?"

"I..." Evelyn slammed the mug down and stormed off.

"There's another reason," Shawn said, looking in the direction Evelyn had gone in. "I was warned."

Zan gave him an inquisitive look.

"The raven and the man she talked about? I saw the raven anyway, I think, in my dreams. And Raven, capital R, is a trickster for my people, and an important spirit. If he's drifting about, nothing *good* is happening, and he feels like he should be involved." He frowned. "I *had* a raven as a passenger coming up, but he seems to have left again."

"And the man?"

They both looked up at a knock on the back door and saw Kal standing there, looking a bit tousled. The wind had started up and there were raindrops beginning to fling themselves at the windows.

"Kal?" Zan said. "What are you doing here?"

"I do work here," he reminded her mildly. "I saw the lights were on and I wanted to ask Evelyn if she minds my going into the basement. I think your uncle stored some of my more seasonal tools down there."

Shawn and Zan glanced at each other. "Evelyn went upstairs," Shawn said. "I can go ask her."

"Please," Kal said and shivered in the doorway until Zan thought to invite him in. He didn't come in too far; he lingered in the small entry way between the back door and the basement and gazed thoughtfully down into the darkness. Zan studied him in turn.

He looked odd.

Zan wasn't a big believer in crystals or Ouija boards, or much to do with the commercialized spiritualism in general, but it was hard to live on the west coast and not get brushed by some of it. She didn't go out of her way to buy the stuff or research it, but she didn't go out of her way to debunk it either and she always trusted her gut.

Right now, her gut told her that the man who stood before her wasn't a man at all, but instead was wearing a form she was being led to see. He *flickered* vaguely in the corner of her eyes and the shadows curled around his shoulders and back, reminding her of a cloak.

Or wings.

Before she could chase that errant thought down, Shawn returned.

"Evelyn's said it's fine," he said, giving Kal a deeply thoughtful look. "She's trying to talk to the boys."

"Thank you," Kal said and went down the stairs. The other two lurked at the top, pretending they were watching the rain outside.

"I don't know anything about him," Shawn muttered. "He claimed to have started working here when Evelyn's uncle was dying, but there's no employment record or anything about him."

Zan chewed her lip. "And we're letting him in her *house?*"

Shawn sighed.

Kal must have reached the basement because there were no more sounds of creaking stairs, but as the minutes ticked by, there were no sounds of anything else either. They listened with all their might, but only dead air met them.

"We should go check on him," Shawn said.

Zan glanced up as though trying to spot Evelyn through the ceiling, but there was no sign of her either and she sighed. "Yeah," she said. "Hold on." She went back into the kitchen and came back with one of Evelyn's knives. Shawn's eyes widened. "Just in case."

He shook his head, but they both went down the stairs, still listening for Kal.

When they got the basement floor, they heard a small crash from the butcher room and then a grunt of what sounded like pain.

"He must have dropped something," Shawn offered tentatively, but Zan shook her head.

"How could he have gotten in there? The door should be locked."

The butcher room door was indeed wide open and there were now the sounds of pained gasping and clinking. The pair glanced at each other and Zan took point, brandishing her knife, though she wasn't sure whether she'd actually be able to use it if things came to a head.

The butcher room yawned ahead of them, and they quickly saw the source of the noise: Kal was hanging off the massive hook that normally hung empty from the ceiling. He was squirming like a landed fish.

"How did that happen?" Zan said, her mouth open. Kal was dangling, blood dropping down his shoulder, and his hands were firmly bound to the hook above his head.

"How do we get him *down*?" Shawn said, and Zan felt stupid for her initial question.

"Be... ware," Kal gasped, but Shawn darted forward anyway and grabbed the other man to steady him. Blood slithered down his leather coat and under the harsh light of the room, it seemed to shimmer.

"Beware of what?" Zan asked, holding the knife even more tightly. But Kal's breath was coming in pained gasps, and he couldn't answer.

Then Zan felt something unseen slam into her. It sent her staggering back through the door which slammed shut, locking the two men inside.

***

Evelyn immediately felt childish upon leaving the kitchen, but it was too late to go back and apologize. She wasn't even sure *why* she had felt that flash of rage, but it dissipated as quickly as it had arrived. She went upstairs instead. Shawn came a moment later and asked her something, but she said yes to his question, mostly to get rid of him as quickly as she could.

Then she saw Simon peering around the door at her.

"Mom?" he said tentatively. She must have still looked angry or exhausted, but she schooled her face into something more neutral. He didn't exactly look at ease, but at least he looked less worried.

"Good morning," she said, trying to inject cheer into her voice. "Ready to help clean the attic today?"

He wrinkled his nose and shook his head. "Last time we opened the attic door, there was that... thing..."

"I know," she said. "But Zan and Shawn are both here and they can help. And maybe we imagined it. We were all pretty spooked that night, even before I went into the attic."

He looked extremely dubious about that, but he couldn't exactly argue the point either. "Shawn's here?"

"He came to talk to us about selling the house."

She felt oddly gratified to see the same look of anger ripple over her son's face at the suggestion, and then couldn't figure out why.

"I thought we were going to live here forever," he said sullenly.

"Stay forever!"

She buried the voice that slithered pleasantly in through her mind. It sounded like an older man. *"My grandchildren deserve a safe place to have a home, don't you think?"*

"We can't stay here forever," she forced herself to say. "You and your brother have to go back to school in a few weeks and I have to find a new job. This was always just going to be a holiday, remember? And your dad is down south too."

"I don't care about any of that," Simon said.

"Well, we still need to eat and pay the bills," she said as lightly as she could manage. "And there's no work for me up here. And none of your friends are here either. So, we need to finish cleaning up and then sell the place so that we can buy a place closer to everyone we care about."

She wasn't surprised when he slammed the door in her face which prompted Christopher to peer out of *his* door at her.

"I'm glad we're leaving soon," he said quietly. "I don't like it here."

It was easier to swallow the rage when faced with her youngest son. "I know," she said. "We'll move back home soon."

"Will Shawn move too?"

She laughed. "I doubt it. His family all live here. And his work is here too."

He looked a little sulky at that, but unlike his brother, he came out and went downstairs.

"Mom, where is Shawn and Zan?" he called and Evelyn came downstairs. "You said Shawn was here."

"Maybe they went outside," she said, putting out some cereal for him.

"It's *raining*," Christopher protested, and Evelyn shrugged. He stood up and looked out the kitchen window, and then returned to his seat. "They're not there."

Evelyn frowned and was about to set forth another theory when she heard a shout from the basement.

"That's auntie Zan!" Christopher said, his eyes wide.

"Stay here," Evelyn said and headed for the basement stairs. Christopher looked as though he was going to follow her, but she scowled at him, and he sat back down. "I'll be right back. Zan probably just tripped."

Christopher didn't look satisfied with this answer, but also knew he wasn't going to be allowed to go with her, so he sat down, and Evelyn made her way down the stairs.

"Zan!" she called. "Are you okay?"

"Evelyn!" Zan shouted back. "I need your help."

Evelyn darted down the steps as quickly and safely as she could and saw Zan standing in front of the butcher room, banging on the door. She had the beginnings of a bruise on her shoulder, but she was ignoring it. "Kal and Shawn are locked in there and Kal's hurt."

"How?" Evelyn asked. "That door is looked."

"And now we need the key," Zan said. "Hurry!"

Evelyn carried the keys with her to keep the boys from stealing them to get into rooms they shouldn't be getting into. She took them out and fitted the butcher room key to the lock. It jammed part way and she had to wrench it to get the lock to sullenly give. The door swung open and Zan dashed inside.

"Shawn!" she called, and he turned around.

"What happened?" he asked. Kal was no longer hanging by the hook, but he still looked terrible. "I got him down, but the door refused to open and it's *freezing* in here."

Evelyn didn't feel cold, but Shawn's lips were tinged blue, and his teeth were chattering. Kal was wobbling on his feet and there was a strange stain down his leather jacket that glimmered in the light.

"Evelyn to the rescue," Zan said, ushering them both out to the much warmer basement.

"What are you *all* doing down here?" Evelyn demanded.

"I did tell you that Kal was here to get some tools," Shawn pointed out and Evelyn waved a hand. "We heard a noise and came down here to investigate. We found him... tied to that meat hook. How did that happen?"

Kal grimaced as he held his hand over his shoulder. "I came down here looking for my garden shears and thought they might be in the butcher room. It wasn't locked. But something grabbed me, stabbed my shoulder, and then tied me to the hook" He shook his head. "It hurts."

"I'll drive you to the hospital," Shawn said. Kal held up a hand and they stared at him.

"Not a hospital," he said. "I can't go to a hospital. I just need someone to bandage this properly."

"Are you *insane*?" Evelyn demanded. "You're *bleeding out*."

"Help me get out of here," Kal said, ignoring her and making his way towards the stairs. "This place isn't helping."

"Something shoved me out of the room too," Zan said uncertainly as Shawn helped Kal navigate the stairs. "Nearly sent me across the room."

"That butcher room is an epicentre of blood," Kal said. "Darkness lies there."

"Delirious," Shawn mouthed over his shoulder, but the two women shook their heads at him. Zan could well believe that something dark was all throughout the house, but Evelyn could only feel the presence of her father defending his home.

Shawn helped Kal into the kitchen and Evelyn shooed a curious Christopher to his room to play. Kal sat heavily on one of the chairs and carefully moved his hand out of the way. It was covered in blood, but it still looked strange even in proper lighting.

Even odder, the wound had already stopped bleeding and when Evelyn looked closer at it, the edges of the hole seemed to be faintly glowing. She shook her head and rubbed her eyes, but the glow remained.

"What's going on?" she asked, looking up at Kal. He met her blue eyes with his strange gold-flecked ones and suddenly she felt as though she was falling in light, feeling the brush of feathers all around her and the faint sound of bells.

This is not how I intended you to find me, came a voice from all around her. *My mask has been weakened by the enemy. But I can make you forget.*

No!

Something seemed to deeply studying her and the feathers pressed in more closely.

Be not afraid.

Light bloomed around her and she saw a mass of black feathers and golden eyes staring at her. For a moment, she felt warm, bathed in light, but then the warmth turned to uncomfortable heat and the light pierced through her until her mind couldn't take it anymore and her consciousness fled. Behind her, she was sure she heard her father shout in fury and the golden light winked out.

"What happened?" Zan shouted as Evelyn collapsed out of her chair. Shawn bolted up as well and glared daggers at Kal, who held up his hands. Zan pulled back her eyelids, but she was completely unresponsive.

Kal crouched beside her and put a hand on her forehead as though checking for a fever. Zan nearly swatted his hand away, but then she saw Evelyn's eyes start to open of their own accord.

"Evie, are you okay?" she asked. Kal moved a bit to let her in Evelyn's line of sight.

"My head," she grunted and narrowed her eyes against the gray light coming in through the window. She did a full body shudder as though trying to rid herself of her own skin and then, with Zan's help, regained her chair. But Zan noticed that her eyes kept sliding over to Kal and whenever she saw him, she did another full body shiver.

Kal sat back down in his own chair and looked tired. Once she was sure that Evelyn wasn't going to fall again, Zan helped Kal clean up the injury on his shoulder, though the hole already looked as though it was healing on its own. She shook herself.

"You," Evelyn finally said, staring straight at Kal. "You aren't what you seem."

He stared back at her. "Are any of us?"

"I *remember*," she hissed, standing up. Shawn grabbed her hand to no avail. "The feathers and the eyes and the *judgement*."

"I'm sorry," Kal said, though he didn't look sorry. "It's built into what I am. Rather like hormones and blood are built into what *you* are."

"What are you talking about?" Zan demanded, now staring at Kal as well. She had stopped cleaning his wound.

"He's an angel," Evelyn said flatly.

Zan stared between them and then snorted and went back to patching up Kal. "No such thing," she proclaimed. "And I never figured you for the religious sort."

"I'm *not*," Evelyn said. "And anyway, I don't mean those silly cherubs or fawning women with big white wings you see on paintings. I mean the *real thing*. Old Testament, smiting, judgement. Turning people into pillars of salt."

"That wasn't me," Kal said mildly, a half smile on his features. "And I have little intention of smiting anyone here, even if I could." The smile twisted on itself. "I'm not sure I have the ability to smite anyone anymore. I'm hardly here by choice."

"I suppose that makes you a fallen angel," Zan scoffed, but Kal grimaced.

"I'm not *Infernal*," he said. "Just... asked the wrong questions of the wrong sorts, I suppose. I wouldn't say that I completely agree with the Morningstar, but I do find you humans to be... strange."

Zan threw her hands in the air. "So, you're telling me it's all real? That there is a God and angels and heaven and hell?"

Kal gazed at her, and his eyes seemed to start swirling through amber, blue, gray, and green until Zan had to look away.

"One of your writers said, 'Hell is what you make it'," he said quietly. "God and heaven are too. For myself, they were my brothers and sisters, to use your words. To you, they may be nothing more than mist, a dream that dissolves upon waking." He spread his hands. "I wouldn't tell you what is real and what is not. You humans build your own reality every minute of every day. Free will and choice are the most important things you have. So, I'm not going to tell you either way. Believe what you will, or don't. But I am here to help you, not harm you."

There was a sudden bang on the window, and they all looked out to see a large raven perched on the window ledge, peering in with a bright eye. Evelyn yelped in surprise, but Shawn got up and stood in front of the window.

"It's the same raven that came here with me," he said. "I recognize the markings on his head. But what is he doing here?"

"I think he wants inside," Kal noted dryly. He flinched as Zan tied off the bandage, but otherwise continued studying the bird.

"Birds don't normally act that way," Zan said, helping Kal get his leather jacket back on.

Kal gave her a wry look. "And houses aren't generally haunted, and angels don't generally reveal themselves to humans." He got up and opened the window, letting the massive black bird hop daintily inside. He dodged around Shawn and the sink and came to rest in the middle of the table where he began preening his wings.

"Honoured Raven," Shawn said tentatively. The raven looked up at that and winked an eye before going back to the work of drying his feathers. Zan swallowed hard.

"You don't like birds?" Shawn asked.

"I like them fine," Zan said. "Just not on the kitchen table."

The raven gave her a wicked look and squatted slightly. She slapped her hands towards the bird and it cawed merrily, moving out of her reach.

"Ravens and crows are very clever," Shawn said. "Tricksters. But they should still be polite." He gave the bird a stern look and, surprisingly, he seemed vaguely embarrassed by his conduct.

Evelyn shook her head. "You said you were here to help," she said to Kal. "So why haven't you been?"

"Who says I haven't been?" Kal said and she felt a little ashamed. "But now it's time for a more active role. The being that your father became is growing stronger, feeding on fear and the lineage he enticed to return home."

"I dreamed about you," Shawn said suddenly. "You and Raven. You told me I had to help."

"I did too," Evelyn murmured. "That it was up to me to decide."

"Free will and choice are the most potent of all the things in this mortal universe. For good or ill."

"So, what do we have to do?" Zan asked.

Kal looked towards the ceiling. "The basement is where your father conducted his murders," he said. "But the attic is where he dwells now." His strange amber eyes narrowed. "But he makes his foothold elsewhere now, or at least he is making the attempt. We must hurry."

Chapter Twenty-One

Evelyn reluctantly made her way to the attic door in the ceiling and looked up at it. She could swear she saw it starting to bulge out towards her and she rubbed her eyes. Everything was swimming slightly at the edges of her vision, but when she focused, the bulging vanished.

"I know you're up there, dad," she muttered.

No one answered her of course, but she wasn't sure how she felt about that, especially with Kal's warning ringing in her ears.

Footsteps behind her startled her from her reverie and she turned to see Zan. Her best friend frowned at the ceiling panel too.

"I don't like attics," she said. "Never have. They're usually full of dust and spiders."

"This one definitely has dust," Evelyn said. "I only saw a couple really small spiders though."

Zan gave it a fretful look, but Evelyn reached up and pulled the draw string. The ladder came down with a clatter that sent them both jumping backwards.

"Nothing to worry about," Evelyn said, but her voice came out on a squeak. Zan frowned, but she started climbing the ladder first with Evelyn behind her.

Simon's door creaked open, but the two women didn't notice him peering out to see what they were doing.

As they reached the attic, strange shapes showed in their peripheral vision. Zan made her way to the largest piece of furniture and nudged the sheet off, then stopped and stared at what she had uncovered.

"Don't," Evelyn whispered, remembering the woman in the mirror below. But Zan ignored her.

The mirror was tall and ornate, the glass covered in a film of gray dust and dirt, completely distorting her reflection. The frame was wooden and carved with strange whorls and shapes that made her eyes ache when she studied them. Evelyn steadied herself and looked over Zan's shoulder.

"There's a mirror like this in the basement," she said. "And I saw another woman in the reflection."

"There's no one here but us," Zan said firmly. "Once this is cleaned up, it might be worth some money to a collector. It looks old."

Evelyn gave her an uneasy look, but pulled sheets off an old and partly wrecked loveseat, several more boxes of books, some old tires and yard tools, and a large collection of bottles and mason jars, none of them very clean.

"I guess he collected all kinds of things," Evelyn said weakly. There was also the simple debris of a life of accumulated stuff like old shoes, clothing, and coat hangers, and she wasn't sure what to do with any of it.

"We're going to need Shawn's help with some of this," Zan said. "This furniture looks heavy and fragile. And we can't clean anything without more light."

Evelyn drifted over to the round window and rubbed some of the grime away. The thin sunshine strengthened as it came in and dust could be more plainly seen in the air.

"At least there's no spiders yet," Zan said, still looking at the boxes and using the old sheets to dust off anything she could reach. "Or mice."

The sunlight hit the old mirror and made the dust glow. The glow caught both Zan and Evelyn's eyes and for a moment, it was almost peaceful.

Then the mirror bulged.

It happened so quickly that Evelyn and Zan both though they imagined it, but as they took a closer look, they realized that the glass was bubbling out.

"Trick of the light," Zan said, but she didn't sound at all certain, especially when Evelyn dragged her to look at it from one side. The glass was definitely being pushed out.

"Warping?" Evelyn asked, but then the bulge shifted and stretched, turning into grasping fingers that reached for Evelyn, seeming to follow the sound of her hysterical breathing.

"Get back to the ladder!" Zan yelped, dragging her friend backwards. The mirror hand reached and groped, trying to grab Evelyn. They got to the ladder and looked back to see that the mirror had flattened again, and the sunlight had dimmed.

"We must have imagined that," Zan said.

"Both of us?" Evelyn demanded. Her heart was hammering in her chest and she felt as though she couldn't catch her breath.

"We'll... go take a break," Zan said, giving the mirror a mistrustful look. "But we'll be back." She felt like she was threatening the furniture, but of course nothing answered her. They made their way back down and into the kitchen.

Simon looked up at the attic in their wake.

"*Grandson...*"

***

Kal and Shawn had volunteered to clean out the butcher room.

The raven watched them descend the stairs, tilting his head and muttering to himself. He then hopped on top of the banister, his powerful claws flexing in the wood and leaving scratch marks. He rattled his tail feathers as something slimy and dark tried to steal over him, but a warning rattle was enough to send it slinking away.

The Infernals that muttered against the mortals didn't disturb him, but the fact that they were encroaching on his territory did. He could feel the deaths of his children here and it rankled him, made his feathers itch. His fellow spirits hovered at the barrier, demanding he act, but he knew it wasn't *quite* his place and it certainly did not lie in his power to invite the Others in.

Though there was some ambiguity in what his place was and that was where his power lay. After all, a trickster never walked a straight path. He chuckled deep in his throat and made his way back to the kitchen, where he knew he would find at least one silver knife and several bundles of dried sage left by one of his daughters before she had been forced to flee.

"You have no power here, Trickster," oozed a man's voice from above, and he rattled his tail feathers again. *"I did not defile your territory."*

He did not deign to answer. Giving the colonials power by acknowledging them wasn't in his best interest. Instead, he took the knife in his claws, carried the sage in his powerful beak, and began his careful descent down the basement stairs.

Kal and Shawn looked around the main room of the basement, carefully avoiding the butcher room. Unfortunately, there wasn't much to distract them from their target, just an old mirror covered in a sheet.

The butcher room door had been closed again after rescuing Kal. Looking at it was enough to give Shawn a horrible claustrophobic feeling. He glanced at Kal, but if the man (*angel?*) was uncomfortable being near the room where he had been hurt a mere hour ago, he showed no sign. The bandage Zan had wound around his shoulder made his movements a bit stiff, but otherwise he gave no sign of being in pain.

Shawn was racking his brain trying to remember what he had learned about angels, but his family wasn't very religious, save for one older cousin, and everyone ignored her. He didn't even consider himself to be particularly spiritual, but Raven seemed to be following him around anyway. *Can angels be hurt?* He supposed it must be possible since Kal had been, but Kal didn't seem much like what his cousin had tried to tell him about when he was a kid. Aside from feeling as though he was walking by someone with very different experiences to his own, Shawn didn't really feel frightened or awed by Kal.

Opening the door to the butcher room was anticlimactic. Shawn opened it and Kal swept in, but all that happened was that the hanging hook shifted slightly in the breeze created by the door opening. Kal stood in front of the hook and frowned.

"Its attention has moved," he muttered.

"The attic?" Shawn asked, and the raven landed heavily on his shoulder, the knife dropping to the floor with a solid clank. He picked it up and felt the tickle of the sage stuffed in the raven's beak against his ear. "Thank you."

Kal did a slow circuit of the butcher room, but shook his head.

"There are traces here and something perhaps, but not the focus. It's moving around."

Shawn shook his head. "Maybe Evelyn and Zan did something."

They returned to the kitchen and saw that Evelyn and Zan must have been there and gone again: there were a couple of mugs of coffee on the table, still full, but they were abandoned. Then they both heard a crash coming from above and Christopher came flying into the room, looking terrified.

"The attic! Mom and auntie Zan!" he gasped out and Kal sat him down while Shawn hurtled up the stairs, the raven squawking and swaying on his shoulder.

The ladder was down, and the raven hopped off and waited for Shawn to climb it before following him.

The first thing that caught Shawn's eye was Zan's bright auburn hair, a direct contrast to Evelyn's dark waves. Both the women were standing with their backs to him, facing a massive mirror that seemed to be bulging slightly, straining towards them. Shawn gulped down a sick feeling of horror; up to this point, the haunting, such as it was, had been limited to weird noises and events he only heard about after.

This was real.

But the women were equal to it.

Evelyn was slightly in front of Zan, staring at the mirror which no longer looked to have a hand jutting out, but instead faces swirling in the glass. They seemed to be trying to talk to her, but she only had ears for the voice of her father, whispering for her to reach out and touch his hand, to help him save his home.

You miss your old home and your old life, but this place was built for you, little Evie. Come back. Come home.

Her heart ached and the faces of her children swam before her. A home, stability. This was her home, her inheritance, she knew that from the diary, and she had every right to it.

But Zan's warmth beside her reminded her that the price for her inheritance would be too high.

"No," she whispered and pulled away from her father. It hurt and she felt all the childhood wounds open again, but every time her father brought her close to him, she found herself doing something terrible.

The hand in the mirror suddenly lashed out and grabbed her by the throat. Before Shawn could reach her, Zan had snatched up what looked like an antique umbrella stand and smashed it into the mirror.

There was a cacophony of screeching that sounded nothing like breaking glass, then the hand disappeared while shards showered around them.

"Well," Shawn said in the sudden quiet. "That worked."

The raven hopped on the floor and tilted his head on the broken shards of the mirror. Shawn grabbed the sage he dropped and lit some with a match, wafting the smoke around the space. It made everyone sneeze, but it was something of a cathartic release.

"It's not done," Kal said. Shawn jumped: the black-haired man seemed to have appeared from thin air even though he could have sworn Kal had simply climbed up the ladder behind him. His features were still drawn. He studied the broken mirror and shook his head, the sage smoke curling around his shoulders and head.

"The master of the house has a new foothold," he said. "Close."

"Where are the boys?" Zan asked, and Evelyn's face paled. She dodged around the others and nearly tumbled down the ladder in her rush.

"They were both in the kitchen," she hollered behind her, but when she got there, only Christopher was there, and he was sprawled on the floor near the basement stairs. She let out a cry and cradled his head in her lap while Shawn checked his eyes and had her lift him a little so he could check his head.

"Goose egg," he reported. "But I think he'll be okay. Where's Simon? He wasn't here when Kal and I came up here."

The raven hopped to the landing and looked down. A few stray sage leaves speckled his wing, glittering slightly in the weak sunlight.

"The butcher room is the epicenter of the darkness," Kal said. "And that's where the master of the house goes to be reborn." He took off his jacket and laid it over Christopher, who mumbled and then held it closer to him. "It will keep him safe," he explained. "Let's save Simon."

Evelyn took the lead, but Zan hung back a moment, frowning in thought. She seemed to waver there for a moment, and then grabbed something off the kitchen counter and followed her best friend.

The basement yawned in shadow at the bottom of the stairs, but there was light coming from the butcher room. It glimmered on the broken shards of glass from the mirror stored in the big room. Evelyn led the way to the butcher room and shoved the door all the way open.

All four of them stared in horror at the eleven-year-old calmly sitting in the middle of the room, the hook swinging oddly above his head.

"Simon?" Evelyn said first, and then choked a little as though something had struck her throat. "What... are you doing down here?"

"Visiting grampa," he said calmly. He was holding a bone figure in his hands, stroking its head thoughtlessly. "He's the only one who listens to me anymore. Dad hates me, you're too busy, and Shawn and Kal are just idiots." He wrinkled his nose with familiar teenage disdain, though his eyes looked distant and cold. "Grampa says I have to stay here, especially since you rejected him." He smiled a bit. "Just like dad rejected you."

Evelyn lunged to grab her son's arm, but he swayed out of the way and Kal held her back. "He is not your son now," he murmured in her ear. "At least, it is not your son who is speaking."

Zan crossed her arms over her chest. "And what's *my* role in this?"

Simon huffed, but he didn't seem to have an answer and Zan's mouth curled into a dry smile. "No anger for me? But then, how can there be? I'm not related to any of you, and no offense, but I haven't taken sides in any great spiritual mumbo-jumbo. So, your grampa has no insults to lob at me. Listen up kiddo, *kick him out*. He's not your grandfather, he's a monster trying to use you. And you would hate to be *used*, wouldn't you?"

For a moment, Evelyn was sure she saw a flicker of her stubborn and affectionate son in his eyes, but it was frozen over again a moment later. Simon stood up, the hook creating a weird halo over his head. Kal bared his teeth.

"Grampa wanted mom to help him, but she's so useless that he asked me instead," he said scathingly, and Evelyn flinched, clenching her fists. "He is relying on me to keep this house safe forever."

There was a heavy weight on Evelyn's shoulder, and she realized that the raven was perched there, cocking his head towards her. His beak brushed her ear. *"He has been cornered and a cornered, maddened fox will bite. Be careful."*

Evelyn glanced at the raven and saw a few sprigs of sage clinging to his feathers. She grabbed them from him and showed them to her son, who flinched back.

"You screwed up, dad," she said evenly. "Maybe you thought to divide us by coming to this place and straddling between Shawn's people and ours, but you *failed*. Let my son *go*."

Simon's face seemed to twist and change; for a moment, he looked like a much older man, with creases and scars on his face, but then it changed back to her son, albeit with cold eyes. He laughed.

"Those tiny things mean *nothing* to me," he said.

"Do it," Kal said, and the Raven rubbed his beak on Evelyn's ear encouragingly.

Zan whipped out a thick candle from under her jacket, Shawn lit the wick and Evelyn held the sage into the flames. A thick wreath of smoke, far thicker than should have come from so few leaves and such a small fire, billowed forth. It smelled of dry leaves and, strangely, of pure water and summer wind.

To Simon, the effect was immediate and catastrophic. He collapsed to his knees, retching and choking. Evelyn nearly ran to his side, but Kal's arm held her back, firm as a bar of iron. Shawn held her hand.

"Simon," she said, tears running down her face.

"*Discede daemonium,*" Kal intoned and moved forward, his shirt oddly billowing and melting. He pressed his fingers on Simon's forehead, who howled anew and thrashed. The raven began pacing around the boy, his head bobbing slightly, and as he did, the sage fog followed him. Evelyn swore she could see faces in the mist, hissing and spitting at her boy while giving her friendly smiles. They were all young, most of them not much older than nineteen and a couple of them as young as Christopher. Simon flinched back every time one of them came too close, and his face twisted into a snarl, but he couldn't force them away. If anything, the smoke seemed to be slowly moving closer, until it was holding her son in a tight embrace, forcing him to cough and wheeze.

"This is what needs to happen," Shawn muttered to Evelyn, but she only barely heard him. Every instinct drove her to get her son, to get her *child* out of the grip of the vengeful ghosts of her father's victims. She almost broke out of Shawn's grip to do just that and then realized that something was pushing her to do it.

Her father wasn't going to relinquish his hold on his grandson so easily. As she watched, brackish water and black goo seemed to spew forth from her son, bubbling fitfully in front of him while he glared at her.

For a knifepoint moment, everyone was still.

Then the raven knocked the candle out of Zan's grasp and the flame touched the black ooze, causing it to roar to life.

Screams.

Kal grabbed Simon and raced him out of the butcher room, nearly bowling Evelyn over. Simon dropped the bone figure and it burst into flames.

Zan shrieked at the raven who flew out with her in pursuit and then Evelyn found herself being dragged out by Shawn. Christopher had already bolted outside upon hearing the noise and was in tears in the back yard.

"Idiot bird," Kal hissed, but the raven looked unrepentant.

Simon was as stiff as a board in Kal's arms, but he suddenly gave a massive shudder, and looked up at Kal in shock.

"Mom!" he yelled, and Kal immediately put him back on his feet, where he flung himself into Evelyn's arms and burst into tears like his brother.

Zan watched the smoke pour out of the basement door and reached for her phone. She didn't really feel the need to save the house, but appearances had to be maintained.

They knew, though, as they waited in the front yard, shivering in the mountain breeze, that Jason had failed in preserving the house his father had built and infected with his darkness.

Epilogue

Autumn came suddenly in the mountains.

Overnight, it seemed, the temperatures dropped, the leaves began turning golden red and orange, the bears grew fat and sleek, and the berries on the mountain ash trees hung brilliant orange, tempting the birds.

Her father's house was destroyed. The firetrucks had a difficult time ascending the rocky driveway and by the time they arrived, the roof had caved in a shower of sparks and flames, the walls bowing under their own weight. The trees were blackened all around, though fortunately the firefighters arrived in time to keep the fire contained to the house and yard. When Evelyn returned to survey the damage for herself, only the stone foundation and a gaping maw of the basement remained. The metal walls and tables of the butcher room were twisted, melted, and charred.

She would only be able to sell the land and she wasn't sure she wanted to do that. Let it all fall to the animals and trees to finish the job of driving out her father's wrath and evil.

Something crunched from the trees, and she looked over to see Kal picking his way towards her. His brow was knit in concentration as he avoided the still-precarious ruins. She waited for him, arms crossed, until he was standing beside her. A final gust of wind flared his coat around his waist, ruffled his dark hair, and then was still.

A huge raven landed on his shoulder, making him wince. The bird opened his beak in a mocking parody of a smile.

"Did it work?" she asked, and he knelt, forcing the raven to awkwardly hop down.

"Whatever evil your father wrought here is fading," Kal said after a moment. "Fire is cleansing, no matter where the darkness attempts to hide."

The raven pecked his way over to where the foyer used to be. He shuffled around the shreds of carpet and wood until he came out with a twisted knot of bone and thread, which he brought back to Kal and dropped into his waiting hands.

"What is that?" Evelyn asked.

"The idol your son was holding," Kal said. He studied the twisted bone for a moment, and it melted between his fingers. He stood up, brushing dust off him. "*Now* it's over. That was the last bit of your father. It's unlikely he could have used it for anything, but still."

"Smart bird," Evelyn said.

"You'll inflate his already swollen ego," Kal said and the bird puffed his feathers.

"Aren't *I* and my boys the last piece?" Evelyn asked. "Blood wills out, as they say."

"*Choices* will out," Kal said. "You can choose to follow your father and blame your ancestry for any atrocities you commit, or you can choose to break the chain he tried to bind you to. Same for your sons."

The raven gave her a beady stare and took to the air to circle and land on Kal's head. He sighed.

"What about you?" she asked. "Are you able to go... home? Where *is* home?"

He looked past her into the mountains and shrugged. The raven seemed to laugh.

"My Father will call me home... Or not... as He sees fit," Kal finally said. "In the meantime, there are always more questions to ask and more mortals to aid. More demons to fight." He gave her a long look and the raven fluttered his tail feathers. "You could do good with your experience. You've been touched and, once so marked, you'll never mistake it in others."

She laughed dryly. "I'm no exorcist or whatever," she said. "And anyway, no one is going to pay for that."

"You'd be surprised," he said, stretching and dislodging the raven, who huffed at him and spiraled back for the nearest tree that could bear his weight. "Perhaps speak to Shawn and his family about the work they have done. You could learn a lot."

She frowned. "I have to go back south. School for the boys and work for me."

He nodded and seemed to flicker. This time, Evelyn was sure she could see massive dark wings. He pulled out a feather and handed it to her, along with what looked to be one of the raven's neck feathers. "If you do decide to set on the path of exorcism, and you need our help, set our feathers to water. We will hear you and come."

She took the feathers and studied them. They were both jet black, but the raven's small one was soft and light, while Kal's much longer one was more like a decoration wrought from velvet over steel. She looked up to thank them, but they had vanished.

She made her slow and thoughtful way back to the car at the end of the driveway to return to her boys and her life.

Behind her, the final chunks of rubble tipped to the ground. It sounded like a dying gasp.

End

Land Acknowledgement

I would like to acknowledge that *Inheritance* takes place on the traditional and unceded territory of the Ts'msyen people. Thank you for the work you have done to preserve your land, language and culture. T'oyaxsut 'nüün. Thank you.

Author's Note

"Okay, so where *did* this come from?" I can hear you say. And it's certainly a change from my usual William Tenys (yes, I'll get back to him! Much to his chagrin).

When I was a kid, I used to love telling ghost stories. I didn't like horror movies or anything like that, but I did like telling spooky stories and scaring my friends. And this has continued through my adulthood – I enjoy reading spooky stories with lots of paranormal influence. I don't need a lot of gore or slasher and I prefer my baddies to be more supernatural (enough human baddies in the world as is!)

So, you could say that *Inheritance* is a throwback to my childhood love of telling ghost stories. But it is also my love letter to the northwest coast.

I moved to Gitanyow, BC when I was 14. I only lived there for four years before moving to Prince George for university, but I loved the mountains, the incredibly fresh air, and the art. And my husband used to tell me *ghost stories* from the Gitxsan people. We'd lie in bed, and he'd tell me about spirits and hauntings, the burning of sage, and how some places never really got cleansed quite right, no matter what anyone did.

So those things stuck in my hindbrain for many years until I sat down last year attempting to write first a paranormal women's lit, which then morphed into a ghost story that crossed some of the lore and history of the Pacific northwest coast (Raven, a nasty spirit that the elders tried to drive out with the burning of sage and other rituals, the more chilling human problems of the higher rates of suicide, drug use, alcoholism, and the Highway of Tears), with the lore of the Colonials (As Raven would put it): angels, a demonic entity, sacrifices, and ghosts.

On top of being a ghost story, I wanted to shed some light on things like the Ts'msyen language (Tsimshian as they are also known, but the actual name is Ts'msyen), the life of many Indigenous people living on reservations, and what life is like in rural northwest BC. (Minus the ghosts and demons... well, I hope!)

And so here we are!

I hope you enjoyed *Inheritance*, maybe got a little creeped out, and learned a little of the Sm'algyax language (I had a lot of fun looking up common words and phrases!)

***

I would like to gratefully acknowledge the work done by Brendan Esom of the Gitga'at First Nations in continually compiling words in the Sm'algyax language and making his work completely accessible to all via the website: https://www.smalgyaxword.ca, as well as the work done by Ts'msyen Sm'algyax Language Authority (https://www.smalgyax.ca/) for compiling and teaching basic grammar, phrases and greetings.

Sm'algyax was the language originally spoken by the Ts'msyen people who lived for thousands of years on the northwest coast of British Columbia, centered around the area of Prince Rupert, Port Simpson, Kitkatla, Terrace, and even going as far as Alaska. In the 1880s until well into the 20th century, speaking and teaching the language was forbidden, devastating the culture, oral traditions and beliefs of the First Nations in the area. Today, the language is mostly spoken by elders over the age of seventy who are trying to save it by teaching it to others in schools, and the work of people like Brendan who compile words and phrases into websites and apps for anyone to access and learn.

Destroying language is one of the ways that colonisers retained their grip on the Indigenous people of BC; by claiming the old languages and teaching them to the next generations, many First Nations are also reclaiming their culture and history. Although I'm a descendant of colonisers myself, I hope that by including the small amount I did here, I can help promote the work that the Ts'msyen people are doing to bring their language back.

Printed in Dunstable, United Kingdom